THE NEGATIVE SOCIETY

MARSHALL LAMM

Fulton Books, Inc.
Meadville, PA

Published by Fulton Books 2019

ISBN 978-1-63338-941-0 (paperback)
ISBN 978-1-63338-943-4 (hardcover)
ISBN 978-1-63338-942-7 (digital)

Printed in the United States of America

This book is dedicated to Luis A. Nunez, lifelong
friend, confidant, and godfather to my son; and my
family, extended family, and too many friends to list.
Last but not least, the Squires of SW Los Angeles.

Introduction

I first began to think about this book in the early 1980s when I started to notice a change in the mentality of the media and the population in general. The recession of the early 1980s hit some Americans very hard, and the print and broadcast media were predicting the end of the comfortable lifestyle in America. I was somewhat surprised since most people I knew did have to cut back, some were struggling, and some suffered significant losses. I also noticed that all of them seemed to recover and flourish once the recession ended. I was in my early thirties at that time, and I was part of the workforce that was laid off, and I admit that I had a rough time financially. Still, I always seemed to find a way to eat and pay my bills (although late in many cases). I took note of the fact that people continued to improve their lot in life over the next thirty-five plus years despite several recessions and the constant political turmoil present in Congress. Some of the improvements were driven by new technologies that impacted a majority of the population, such as personal computers, wireless communications, satellite TV, etc. Some of the individual improvements came from the simple fact that we improve our lot in life as we grow older and progress in careers and earn more money. I looked around during all these years and noticed that the lot of the average American was improving every year, despite some setbacks along the way.

I clearly remember growing up in the 1950s and 1960s, and what was considered the middle class in those years has made improvements in leaps and bounds since that time. Not only did the lifestyle improve, but it expanded to include minorities who, during the 1950s and 1960s, were largely excluded from the "equal" opportunity for the pursuit of happiness. Today, I am proud to say, people of all backgrounds are seeing their lives improve, the opportunity for their children improve, and their opportunity to participate in corporate and political arenas expanding daily.

Health and lifespan continue to see improvements as we eradicate or control infectious diseases, discover new surgical techniques that save lives, and have improved dietary choices that lead to better health and vitality.

So why do we think that everything is so bad today? I believe it is because we like absolutes rather than an analysis of any situation. The media and political groups add to this negative mentality by forcing or attempting to make all of us chose sides rather than suggest a reasonable compromise that may satisfy all parties. This negative mentality drives divisiveness and the "us versus them" agenda. It is easier to formulate our opinions based on a source we like, and we take what they say to be true. I have found that even with those I like, I sometimes disagree with their opinion or conclusion and, upon doing further research, found that they are sometimes wrong (like all humans).

This all leads me to why I wrote this book. I take a look at a number of topics today that tend to divide people and tried to discuss them as I understand them. I do not want everyone to agree with the positions I outlined. I would only ask that those who do read this text will think about what is said or reported. I encourage disagreement and civil discussions to discuss any topic, as that is the fabric of our nation. People that disagree with me are not idiots; neither are those that agree. I know that over the course of my life, I have changed my position on a number of issues. I did so because I was presented with a logical reason supported by data and/or personal experience. The key is the ability to listen, discuss, agree, or disagree and still respect the other party. This country was founded on the premise that we can disagree on issues and still live together in harmony. I see this every day in life because people are too polite to aggressively attack other's opinions in a face-to-face situation. The advent of social media has provided an opportunity for individuals to publically ridicule others without fear of retribution. This, in turn, leads people to believe that life in America is full of strife and confrontation when in fact it is not as 326 million people coexist every single day.

Reading this book, I hope that you will consider all points and topics and make your own decision on your personal position. *Do not* let anyone convince you that your opinion is any less valuable than any other. We are all adults, educated in schools and life, and are fully capable of forming our own opinions. What I would ask is that we also recognize the validity of other opinions even if we disagree with their conclusion. If a majority of the population takes one side that you do not support, it does not mean that you should continue the fight forever. Accept the decision of the majority but pay close attention to prevailing opinion going forward as public opinion can change over time, and we should revisit previous decisions when this shift takes place. There are numerous examples in the past and are present today. Civilized discourse is healthy for any republic, and a civilized society can't exist without the willingness to agree to disagree.

I hope you enjoy reading this book as much as I enjoyed writing it. The country and the world is not worse now than in the past, and predictions of future apocalypse are no more valid than they have been in the past. Our country and the world are more prosperous, healthy, and safe than at any other time in history. I would hope you would agree with that assessment once you finish reading, but I will respect your opinion if you don't.

Race

If the mainstream and even secondary media outlets, along with so-called experts are to be believed, race relations in the United States have not progressed over the last six decades. Report after report highlights an instance where someone was profiled, refused service, denied access, or otherwise isolated due to their race. This, the critics claim, is proof that America is a racist country. Is this really true? Have the efforts of our civil right icons led by Dr. Martin Luther King Jr. and others been for naught? Let's take a look at some realities in our society today.

Every day in America over 326 million people get up and go to work, school, church, sporting events, and shop without incident. They live together in neighborhoods, develop friendships, and associate with each other without concern for racial makeup. All the old "Jim Crow" laws have been repealed, and tolerance for racial bigotry has all but vanished from the American landscape. I speak to nearly everyone I meet, whether a casual meeting in a line at the grocery store, sitting next to someone at a sporting event or entertainment venue, or passing them on the sidewalk, or in a more formal setting such as work and political events. The common denominator in all these scenarios is that there is no difference in the responses I get from any of the people, regardless of race. Some smile and respond with a "good morning," others nod, and on rare occasions others say nothing. It only reinforces my position that all races want to get along, provide for their families, and live a happy life. Isn't that the essence of life in America?

The definition of the terms racism and racist have evolved in today's society to label anything that a particular group does not support. A word or phrase can make you a racist. Support of a certain agenda can be labeled racism. The simple fact is racism is an act. Denial of rights or opportunities due to race is racism. Yelling racial slurs at an individual is racist. If people will admit the truth, almost everyone in America has likely had a racist thought at some time or another. This does not make them racist! I have a black friend named Kenneth who served with me in the Marines, worked at the same company, and hung out with me socially come to my house in Los Angeles in 1972 to watch a football game. He brought another of his friends with him. We were enjoying the game, drinking a couple of beers, and enjoying the afternoon when his friend commented, "I don't usually like white people, but you're a cool dude." Kenneth practically lost it, telling his friend, "How can you embarrass me and my friend with such a racist comment?" I did not think this individual was a racist as he was very cool with me, and he was merely relaying his experiences. It turns out he had very limited interaction with whites at that time. He was complimenting me in his mind, and I viewed it as such. Do I think he was a racist? No, because he clearly was comfortable with me, and more exposure to others would certainly enlighten his perspective. He was merely a product of his environment at a time when civil rights and integration were just becoming a reality in our society.

Racism is not limited to a single race. It is practiced worldwide by a shrinking minority in all races. This fact is usually overlooked by the media outlets in the USA. Acts of racism by nonwhites are explained away by justifying it as a result of past racial injustice. Racism is racism regardless of the individual or group that practices it. Fortunately for America, those who practice racism are a shrinking minority in all racial groups in the country as the truth of civil rights leaders in history from Gandhi to Martin Luther King Jr. rings true and is accepted as such by the vast majority of all races. As a young man living in Los Angeles, I lived in a neighborhood that was mostly black. I had a neighbor, an older gentleman, who would sit out on his front porch most afternoons. One day I was walking back from the liquor store with a six pack of beer when this gentleman asked if I had an "extra" beer I could spare. I responded that I didn't have an extra but I would certainly share one with him. To add perspective, during the 1970s I was in my twenties with long hair and rode a chopped motorcycle (and personally experienced discrimination as a result). We talked about sports, motorcycles, music, and other topics normally discussed in casual conversation. He also had a young granddaughter that lived with him who was around seventeen years old. He told me that he didn't have anything against me but advised me to stay away from his granddaughter (she was very attractive). Although there is no doubt that this was a racist attitude, it did not make him a racist. He did not hate me, resent me living next door, or shun me socially as we became friendly over the time I lived next door. He was simply expressing the attitudes he was taught growing up in the early twentieth century. His granddaughter did want to go for a ride on my chopper, and I asked his permission before agreeing to do so.

There are others who believe that racism exists in events limited by race, and their arguments are compelling. Is the Miss Black America contest racist? Is Miss Hispanic USA racist? Is Miss Asia USA racist? Is 100 Black Men of Atlanta a racist organization? Is the drive to support traditionally black colleges racist? My answer is no, although a good argument can be made to say yes. The issue that drives people to point out these organizations and others that identify by race is the fact that any attempt to have the Miss White America, 100 White Men of Atlanta would be protested violently and labeled racist. I see nothing wrong with racial pride as long as it doesn't position itself to be superior to others. Some of these organizations, like 100 Black Men of Atlanta, do many valuable services in the community to foster education, mentoring, and guidance for the youth of Atlanta. This is clearly not a bad thing. In reality a society without racial bias would not need separate events or organizations. They are acceptable to me if they push a positive agenda and support other similar organizations representing other racial groups.

Unfortunately, in our current political climate, both parties, Democrats and Republicans, try to use race to political advantage. The Democrats claim that they are the party of minorities in America. The Republicans claim that they have done more to support the rights of minorities. Neither party is free of acts that did not advance racial equality. The Democratic party supported slavery (as did some Republicans), introduced Jim Crow laws, and founded the Ku Klux Klan.

In 1956 J. William Fulbright, a man celebrated by President Bill Clinton in 1995 as a man who stood against the twentieth century's most destructive forces, signed the "Southern Manifesto" along with ninety-nine other senate Democrats and two senate Republicans from Virginia that opposed Brown v. Board of Education and documented their commitment to segregation forever. In 1964 Senator Fulbright participated in a filibuster of the Civil Rights Act of 1964 that lasted eighty-three days. In 2010 the senate president pro tempore was Robert Byrd D-WVa, a former exalted cyclops of the Ku Klux Klan. When MSNBC was commemorating the fiftieth anniversary of George Wallace's "Stand in the School House Door" stunt, the network identified Wallace as R-Ala when he was a member of the Democratic Party. It is only fair to point out that Fulbright, Byrd, and Wallace all renounced their racist beliefs, more so to further their political careers in my opinion than a true enlightening. Speaking of the Civil Rights Act of 1964, the votes by party are not what most would expect:

> House Democrats—61 percent in favor
> House Republicans—80 percent in favor
> Senate Democrats—69 percent in favor
> Senate Republicans—82 percent in favor

Don't think that the Republicans are exempt from racially insensitive acts. Even though they were the party that abolished slavery, passed anti-lynching laws, Civil Rights Act of 1875, 1957, 1960, and 1964, they were hardly the model of tolerance on racial matters. The support for "law and order" in the Republican party led to a blind eye toward racial profiling and interaction between police officers and minority citizens. We can all see evidence of this result when looking at videos present today that clearly show mistreatment of minorities by some police officers. The Rodney King beating was the first of these videos to go viral and open America's eyes to the different experiences of minority citizens when compared to whites.

The zero-tolerance drug laws of the 1980s to combat cocaine trafficking was unfairly applied in the minority communities, resulting in the incarceration of minorities at a much higher rate than in the white community as district attorneys in more affluent (and predominately white) communities were much more willing to plea bargain to lesser charges to allow young offenders to avoid mandatory sentencing guidelines. In 1971 in Los Angeles, California, I was in a car with five black Marines when we got pulled over by LAPD. This particular officer was rude, unprofessional, and clearly had racist attitudes. I made a comment to this officer, and he told me to "Shut up, you're just a white nigger as far as I'm concerned." Please understand that this was 1971, and even at that time, the vast majority of police officers did not represent the same attitude as this individual. It was, however, tolerated by those in power at the time.

Another common tactic by our political leaders is to play the race card in support of their agendas. If the Republicans introduce legislation that reduces government benefits, such as food stamps, welfare, and like government programs, they are immediately labeled as racist and trying to destroy the minority community. This completely ignores the fact that there are as many whites (39 percent) on welfare as blacks (39 percent), and Hispanics numbers (16 percent) are half of the total of white or black. The real cause of the welfare distribution is economics. I further discuss this issue in the chapter on economics. In 2012 there were 12,800,000 welfare recipients in the USA at a total cost of $131.9 billion. That figure translates to a $404 tax burden per person or $948 per working person in the country.

On the other side if Democrats introduce legislation to provide educational support for minorities to gain skills needed to get off welfare, the Republicans cry reverse discrimination despite the fact that education and training is the only real solution to breaking the welfare dependency in poorer communities.

Why aren't the political parties trumpeting the major successes of the civil rights movement? I grew up in the 1950s and can clearly remember the segregation laws of that time. I, personally, did not attend a school with black students until I was in the seventh grade. I remember drinking fountains with signs that read "whites only," lunch counters that would not serve nonwhites, movie theaters that allowed black patrons to only sit in the balcony, and can recall remarks made by adults that were racially offensive but accepted as truth by many. These attitudes were pervasive in all aspects of American life. Blacks were not viewed as having the intelligence to handle top positions in government or business. The success of the civil rights movement has been responsible for black politicians being elected to the highest offices, appointed to the supreme court, starting very successful businesses, and assuming leadership roles in businesses and communities that benefit all. The simple fact of the matter is that both parties try to use race to further their own agenda. They don't want people on both sides of the political divide to look around and notice that the civil rights movement has simply been the most successful social movement in the history of the United States and likely the world although I would have to include South Africa and the dynamic leadership of Nelson Mandela during the transition to majority rule in that country.

Why have the surviving key civil rights leaders of the 1960s been marginalized by the public in general? Many people, in all groups, believe that they have "outlived their usefulness" and no longer play a key role in race relations. Nothing could be further from the truth. These leaders, however, do little to deflect these opinions. Let's look at the facts. Martin Luther King Jr. is universally accepted as a great leader and visionary who led the civil rights movement to the great strides made in an openly hostile environment. Yet today those who supported his strategy and put their own lives and freedom at risk are viewed as continuing to divide the races by making statements insinuating that nothing has really changed. Although the likes of Jesse Jackson, John Lewis, Andrew Young, and many others too numerous to mention here have gone on to do great things in and out of the movement; they do not get the recognition they deserve for the brutality, threats, and violence they courageously faced. Part of that is directly related to the fact that they do not point out what has changed with the same energy as they highlight circumstances that haven't changed.

It is time that they took a more positive approach to their own achievements. What would Martin Luther King Jr. have thought if he had lived to see the first black president, the first black chairman of the Joint Chiefs of Staff, and many other blacks in key roles in government, business, and entertainment. Fortunately he did live long enough to see Thurgood Marshall appointed to the Supreme Court giving him a glimpse of what the future would bring. Today would he have thought that they reached "the mountaintop" he described in his famous speech on the steps of the Lincoln Memorial? I'm certain he, as do others today, would feel that there will always be work yet to be done, but I also feel that he would not have been bashful about pointing out the gigantic strides forward. The other downside to making statements that nothing has changed is the impact it has on some younger blacks who do not understand the realities present during the early days of the civil rights movement.

I have heard young black males say what they would have done if that some of the atrocities of the time had happened to them. Little do they know about the power of institutionalized racism that they have never had to experience. My older black friends inform these young men that had they tried to take actions they describe, they would have been shot, lynched, or just made to disappear by those trying to keep Jim Crow laws and segregation alive. Recent articles in the Atlanta newspaper regarding the last mass lynching at Moore's Ford bridge in 1946 quoted an eyewitness (who was ten at the time) who claimed that police officers were involved. No one was ever convicted. The fact that the racial intolerance was enforced by police, and the courts made it extremely difficult for those seeking equality to safely take actions. It was the strategies of Martin Luther King Jr. and other civil rights leaders that won over the American people by bringing these atrocities to light, not by open violent rebellion but by presenting the facts to the American people.

Knowledgeable, young people recognize that those who passively protested and were abused laid the groundwork for the political power of the minority communities of today. I believe that the positive changes that were made should be constantly highlighted so as to never return to the dark days of the past although the success of the movement has made that possibility nonexistent. The reason I say that is simple. People born in the 1960s and later do not see race as any type of inclusive or non-inclusive issue. Interracial dating (illegal then) is commonplace today. Social clubs go out of their way to include those of all backgrounds. Derogatory racial comments are viewed as ignorant, not celebrated. Racism cannot be obliterated any more than greed, hatred, and a host of other negative human emotions, and beliefs can be driven from everyone's heart. Martin Luther King Jr. knew this and led the movement that made racism deplorable. Consider this, look at all the gains made in fifty-seven years (since 1960). A complete reversal of legal discrimination and introduction rights and acceptance in one lifetime. All the civil rights icons still with us should be beaming with pride in their accomplishments!

In sports, blacks were viewed as very athletic but not capable of playing more cerebral positions like quarterback in football or point guard in basketball. To make such a statement today would be ridiculous considering the fact that many all-star quarterbacks today are black, and the greatest point guard in NBA history, Earvin "Magic" Johnson, is black. Nonetheless racial stereotypes in sports lingered far longer than they should have, considering sports was one of the great vehicles used to squash racist attitudes. Jackie Robinson wasn't chosen to be the first black player in the modern baseball era solely because of his talent. Other black stars (Josh Gibson, Satchel Paige) had greater baseball talent. He was carefully screened to ensure that he would be able to withstand the pressure of the milestone. He was very intelligent, had great moral character, and understood what his impact would be on America's view on race.

It did not take long for the other sports to follow the path of integration. Despite this fact, athletes were described differently by broadcasters, who I would say were not racist but were a product of their upbringing. As an example in the 1970s, white athletes were described as "smart" players who made the most of their abilities while black players were described as gifted, "natural" athletes. I remember an NFL interview in the 1970s with a black defensive back who was being asked about Roger Carr, a white wide receiver. The interviewer insinuated that Roger wasn't that fast (he ran a 9.3-second one-hundred-yard dash), and the defensive back replied, "Why don't you get out there and try to cover him if you don't think he's fast?" Today no one would make these types of assumptions. Some athletes are naturally gifted, others make their mark by working hard and playing smart, but it is not defined by race.

Racism is also practiced by some within their own racial group, although this is primarily found in the black community. Many high-achieving blacks have been told that they are trying to "act white" because they speak proper English and/or are successful in school or business. The simple fact is that high-achieving blacks have always been active in society. Free blacks started and ran successful businesses in the 1800s. A recent movie brought to light the contributions of brilliant black mathematicians to America's space program in the 1960s. Were these leaders "acting white" or simply being successful? Fortunately this phenomenon is being debunked by black leaders in the churches and communities throughout the country. I have been privileged to work with many people of color that I deemed extremely intelligent, and I never thought they were "acting white."

The opposite of "acting white" is being "black enough" in today's world. One example would be glorifying thug life by young people and the entertainment world. Are we to believe that all black Americans are "thugs" at heart? Does this attitude further racial tolerance and acceptance? Some legitimate arguments can be made that the popularity of "gangsta rap" has brought the races closer as many young people of all races are fans of the genre. During the early days of rap, I noticed that the genre followed the path of some controversial earlier rock bands who highlighted social injustices. Bands like Crosby, Stills, Nash, and Young, who highlighted the Kent State shootings of unarmed college students by US government troops, were replaced by rappers like Ice-T, NWA, and others who were highlighting the injustices occurring in their neighborhoods. Just like rock music who turned more commercial and shied away from political activism (some didn't), rap music became very commercialized and began to move away (some haven't) from their roots and focused on the "gangsta" lifestyle and mentality.

This has caused many young people (of all races) to try and capture the "gangsta' look and appearance. They harmlessly fantasize about living the life, but it has consequences on occasion when others don't realize the "gangsta" in front of them is simply a young person trying to grow up accepted by their peer groups. I have some say that they watched people cross the street to avoid walking by them as an example of racism. Could it be they thought they were avoiding "thugs" who might cause them harm? That is a self-preservation instinct not necessarily tied to race. I mentioned earlier that in the 1970s, I had long hair and rode a chopper motorcycle. Whenever I would go riding with a group of fellow bikers, I would notice people avoiding contact with us when we stopped for gas or to grab something to eat. It seems all had read stories about biker gangs like the Hells Angels, Outlaws, etc. and assumed all long-haired bikers on choppers were the same.

The same mentality is being applied to those who look "gangsta." I have also noticed that any blacks who support a conservative position on any issue have their "blackness" questioned. Think about that for a moment. Are we to believe that there is only one way of thinking in the black community? The simple fact is that black Americans, like all others, have varying opinions and beliefs. They do not vote or form their opinions based on what someone tells them they should believe. The bottom line is simple: if you are judging people based on their "acting white" or being "black enough," you are the one with the racist attitudes. If you judge people by the way they dress or speak, you are the one with the discriminatory attitudes.

I struggled with the topic of this and the next paragraph as they are both very polarizing topics (the Confederate battle flag and the "N" word). I finally decided that if I did not address them directly, I would be cowing down to political correctness. The Confederate battle flag has been the topic of numerous debates. Both sides to this debate have valid points. The Confederate battle flag was not the flag of the confederacy any more than the "Don't Tread on Me" flag in the American Revolutionary War was the American flag. However, minorities have every right to oppose this flag as it was hijacked by every racist organization in America and flown to represent their cause. Due to this fact, the Confederate battle flag has become the banner of racist organizations in America. During my biker days in the 1970s, I had a patch of the Confederate battle flag sown onto my "cutoff" because I was from Georgia. My black friends at the time did not take offense because they knew that I only viewed it as a regional flag. A few years later when I began to realize the reality of the flag and its connection to racist groups, I removed it from my "cutoff."

The "N" word in all its variants is a very difficult subject. There is absolutely no question that its origin and meaning were very derogatory toward blacks and still is in certain contexts. It was a commonly used word by many in society for hundreds of years. An amazing transformation began to take place in the 1970s when comics like Richard Pryor began to publicize the use of the word in the black community in his comedy act. America was shocked by the revelation that a segment of the black community frequently used this word in a self-descriptive manner. Many people (of all races) denounced Richard and others who used this word in their acts. They felt like he was perpetuating racist attitudes. My opinion was just the opposite. The fact that he brought the word to the forefront diminished its impact and actually created a sense of pride associated with the use of the word in certain contexts. Richard Pryor was introduced to me by several black Marines I served with in the 1970s.

We were at Kenneth's house for lunch one day, and he played Richard's album *That Nigger's Crazy*. I had tears streaming down my face from laughing so hard. I became an immediate fan and bought every album he made during his career. He demeaned racism by making fun of it, embracing the terminology, and shining the light of reality on a serious subject with outrageous humor. Some like Oprah Winfrey have spoken out against his material because of his use of the word (even though she and a friend of hers use a variant in conversations with each other in private). Although I respect her opinion, I do disagree. I and the black Marines I have mentioned on a couple of occasions earlier used the word in reference to each other on a regular basis. I, personally, took pride in the fact that I was included in the group by people I respected and admired. My personal advice would be that this word should not be used, but I do not think that those who do should be ostracized in every occasion. The context in the use of this word is very important in how it will be received.

If you use it as a derogatory term, you can expect to be labeled racist and potentially get your ass kicked. If you are using it as a term of brotherhood with close friends, it will be received as such. The danger here is simple, and I had it happen to me. A very close black friend of mine and I were talking a little trash with each other, and the "N" word was being thrown around by both of us. Afterward, another black person, who was within earshot, approached me and said that she was offended by our comments and the use of the "N" word. I was mortified and apologized profusely and assured her she would never hear me say that again. She was also very understanding and told me that she knew I wasn't using it in a derogatory manner, but the word offended her nonetheless. That is the reason my advice is to avoid its use.

My summary on this subject is simple. The United States of America is not a racist country simply because some racist acts occur. The overwhelmingly vast majority of all Americans do not harbor racist inclinations. We get along every day. We help each other whenever help is needed. Think of the "redneck navy," a bunch of bass fishermen who flocked to Houston during the flooding caused by Hurricane Harvey to help rescue people stranded by floodwaters. Many of those rescued and/or helped were minorities. These men (of all races) did this at their own expense because it was the right thing to do and weren't concerned about the skin color of those they were assisting.

There are way too many examples of all races helping other races in this country to believe that racism is inbred into American culture. For those who disagree, please describe or identify a country you feel is not racist. How about Japan? Russia? China? Germany? Egypt? Iran? Nigeria? Which of these or any other country can compare their ruling bodies at all levels of government with the USA in terms of diversity? It is high time we stopped all the negative rhetoric on race relations and celebrate our status as the world leader in racial inclusion. Please rest assured that this does not mean we should ignore any violations of civil rights, and the USA will continue to work to eliminate racist actions whenever they are encountered.

Media

The media in the United States is one of the primary keys to our freedoms. The founding fathers recognized this fact, and the First Amendment guarantees our right of freedom of speech. What happens when the news media is no longer committed to the search for truth or accuracy in reporting? Should the government get involved and regulate the media? Absolutely not! The control of the press has always been one of the first steps in creating a totalitarian state. This is not done in a sweeping move that everyone would recognize and protest. It is done a little at a time with changes so subtle that the average citizen will not recognize what is happening. Don't misunderstand; I am not saying that there is a conspiracy among the news media to undermine America, far from it.

The problem is all news outlets are businesses driven by the push for profitability. This fact drives the management of the media outlets to focus reporting efforts on items that will increase sales and/or improve ratings. In almost all instances, these items are negative by nature. Don Henley of the Eagles released a song in 1982 titled "Dirty Laundry" that highlighted this trend. This is not to say negative items should not be reported. They most certainly should take the forefront. The national news media, in particular, has a responsibility to focus on issues that impact our national security and freedoms. In many cases they do, but in others, they make headlines more suited to gossip news outlets. They have also taken a more editorial view on all issues and provide their readers and/or listeners with their opinion on topics slanted to gain agreement. Half-truths are now acceptable in reporting. That is presenting your position and leaving out the opposing opinions and any data that may support the other side or damage the position you have taken. Even if the other position is discussed, it is frequently done in a manner as to discredit the validity of the opposing position. Couple this fact with the trend in education to memorize facts presented (more on that in the chapter on education) than to take in the information, analyze and research the data, and form your own opinion, and the population becomes much easier to manipulate.

One of the primary causes of the changes in news reporting, especially on the national level, has been the consolidation of major news outlets. The elimination of competition has limited the viewpoints on any subject. I am not saying that reducing the competition has caused a single viewpoint. In fact what it has done is create extremism on both sides of the topics. Large networks that now control news content ensure that all those in their network support the company line or face consequences. Since these networks also control local affiliates, they are able to take their position to local communities. Neither side reporting on the political spectrum is free from bias. The problem presents itself when a segment of the population will only watch a news outlet that slants issues their way (CNN vs. Fox).

The real solution for the population is to listen to both sides of the issue and formulate your own opinion, which, by the way, is as valid as the opinion of anyone in the media, political arena, or pulpit. In today's digital environment, the broadcast media, both network and Internet, have actually expanded dramatically but unfortunately have not taken the high road as the broadcast media attempted in its early days in the 1950s. The major networks at that time attempted to emulate the print media and their self-imposed standards of accuracy via fact-checking, presentation of data only, and restricting "opinions" to the editorial comments. This was possible due to the limited number of broadcast channels that limited those who reported news to just a few. Today anyone with a computer can establish themselves as a "news" outlet. They create names to make themselves appear to be a professional organization and flood the Internet with their views on issues almost always slanted to their viewpoint. These outlets often make claims that are unsubstantiated and are in many cases false. This creates a very difficult situation for the average citizen to determine what is "real" versus "fake" news.

The print media has undergone a similar transformation as fewer and fewer local newspapers are being published today. This is largely a financial problem due to competition from the Internet and not part of any plan to restrict the newspapers' ability to present the relevant news. The fact is many major cities now have only a single newspaper instead of two or three as in the past. This fact alone limits the varying viewpoints presented to the population. I would also state that I believe that these major newspapers make every attempt to be unbiased in their reporting, but human nature is to put more credibility into things you believe. As a result, most of these papers show some sense of bias. Let's look at some examples.

The tax code overhaul of 2017 is a prime example. The facts show that everyone except the very rich will benefit from this change in the tax code. Nonetheless the media reported the benefit to the rich and corporations as outrageous and made very little attempt to outline the advantage to the average taxpayer. Nancy Pelosi (D-Ca) called it crumbs to the average person. Strong talk from a person living in a multimillion-dollar mansion in San Francisco. Ask those average citizens if they consider a savings of $1,000 a year to be crumbs. The bottom line of the new tax code was the resulting uptick in the economy and subsequent pay raises and bonuses distributed to working-class Americans.

The Second Amendment is under constant fire from the media. They point out the senseless loss of life due to gun violence. The simple fact of the matter is gun deaths pale in comparison to many other causes of death in the United States. The amount of air and print time compared to other causes of death is way out of proportion. Medical errors cause more than 250,000 deaths (Johns Hopkins Medical) in the United States per year compared to gun murders (8,124 in 2014 per FBI crime statistics), yet this problem is not a focus of media attention. Obesity is now responsible for one in five deaths, a 350 percent increase in the last decade, yet our media believes any concern about people's weight is rude as people are "healthy at any size"?

The media moves quickly to identify the weapon used in any mass shooting but does not put together the most common cause of mass shootings, mental illness (more on this later). Let's not fail to mention the largest mass murder in the USA in recent history happened in Oklahoma City, and the perpetrator used fertilizer and kerosene, not guns. In comparison there is little reporting of people successfully using firearms to defend themselves legally. Certainly there is no debate in the need for a firearm in these instances. I would not be fair if I did not point out that the media has been instrumental as a watchdog over an industry like gun manufacturers and distributors in our country, and I would hope that they would continue in this role.

The media also likes to jump onto "causes" and be their champion without checking facts if it "feels" right. A great example is the name of the NFL team in Washington D.C. The Washington Redskins have been the target of lawsuits, attempted restrictions on copyrights that would impact revenue, and media campaigns rebuking the use of the name as offensive to Native Americans. *The Washington Post*, in particular, was very vocal on this topic. I will admit that I had an advantage here as one of my best lifelong friends is a full-blooded Apache. He and I served in the Marine Corps together, were roommates after discharge, and are still friends today. I asked him his opinion on this subject, and he was emphatic that the name Redskins was not offensive to him. I also must note that he does not appreciate "Chief Wahoo" of the Cleveland Indians baseball team as he views that caricature as offensive. He pointed out, however, that the Washington Redskins logo was designed in cooperation with the Red Cloud Athletic Fund located on the Pine Ridge Indian Reservation in South Dakota at the request of former Redskin Head Coach George Allen.

In addition the first head coach, while the team was still in Boston, was a Native American. Finally in 2013, the Associated Press decided to take a poll and discovered that 79 percent of respondents did not think the name should be changed. Another poll of Native Americans, taken by the respected Annenberg Public Policy Center, found that 90 percent did not find the name Redskins offensive.

Adding insult to injury was the fact that multiple high schools on Native American reservations used the nickname "redskins." *The Washington Post* did issue an editorial admitting their error on this subject although they pointed out that 10 percent did find the name offensive. In this country we don't make policy decisions based on the opinions of 10 percent.

The media in our current environment does not have the stomach to report on obvious issues if they believe it may offend a certain segment of society. This mentality undermines the effectiveness of the First Amendment. Take Islamic terrorism as an example. There is no question that these terrorist acts are perpetrated by radicalized Muslims, yet the media is very slow to report that radical Islam is responsible. They look for every excuse to deflect that connection. They believe, or so they say, that reporting it that way would cause harm to all the "peaceful" Muslims. That is like saying reporting on the Branch Davidians in Waco would have caused harm to all Christians. The American population can differentiate between radical and peaceful religious followers of any religion.

The war on poverty is another example of media not reporting on the success or failure as they are concerned that their findings would not be popular in a certain segment of society (the poor). The war on poverty was launched in the 1960s with the goal to eliminate and/or substantially reduce Americans living in poverty. Government programs to provide assistance were launched, and people were provided with housing, food, and medical care. This would seem to be a very positive program, but did it meet its objective? Since the objective was to reduce poverty, the answer is no as more Americans are receiving assistance now than ever before. Why have we not explored viable alternatives? Since poverty is caused by lack of job opportunities for some segments of society, why have we not looked at providing training and job skills for those stuck in a cycle of poverty? Instead we promote increasing benefits while ignoring the fact that this strategy has failed.

How many of you have spent time in any of the poverty-stricken neighborhoods or regions in the country? If you have, you will notice that certain conditions always seem to exist. The first would be the lack of businesses that could provide employment and a path for those living in poverty to escape its clutches. The only businesses found in most of these areas are liquor stores, pawnshops, fast food, and "check cashing" locations. The check cashing locations, in particular, charge ridiculous fees that take advantage of those that use them. Why doesn't the media suggest to the government an incentive program for major companies like Kroger, Ace Hardware, CVS, movie theaters (Magic Johnson led the way here), and other businesses to open locations in these impoverished areas? This program should provide significant tax breaks, to offset any additional cost of operation in these areas, and provide training assistance to the companies involved, fund police presence to ensure safe operation, and require these businesses to hire 95 percent of their employees from within the impoverished region. The benefits would be significant in the communities, and the businesses participating would reap a ton of goodwill for their participation in reducing poverty.

I can hear the feedback now: we can't afford this kind of program! Consider this, if half of the twenty trillion dollars spent in the fifty years since the beginning of the war on poverty had been spent in this way, we would have averaged $400 billion per year, over fifty years, to rebuild the financial structure of these areas. In addition, we would have had $10 trillion invested into those same areas. What would these areas have looked like today if that amount had been invested? This program would provide a lot of incentives for companies to assist in recovery and increase their sales. Please do not misinterpret my point on this subject. This country definitely must ensure that the people who genuinely need assistance to survive be given aid. Elderly, disabled, medically challenged people who cannot work must not be ignored. Unfortunately, many recipients of benefits are those who do not fall into one of these categories. If we really want to win the war on poverty, we must provide opportunities for people to work their way out, and if history is any example, they will.

Despite examples like those above, the media in America provides an invaluable service to the country. Their ability to report issues, whether influenced by politics, money, or political correctness, without censorship must never be infringed if we are to maintain our freedoms. It is up to the citizens of this country to force the media to be more objective in reporting and to focus on topics that are truly impacting our country and the world. How can this be done, you ask? I am just a single voice and can't make a difference. Nothing could be further from the truth in today's media environment. In the age of instant access to electronic media by almost all citizens, your voice most definitely can be heard. The issue is that many people need to be engaged. I frequently hear from friends on both sides of the political spectrum that they don't like the methods used when reporting. Too frequently they claim that the media avoids the real issues while focused on "tabloid" reporting, such as a focus on who said what, who was offended, and other issues that do not impact our society. When I ask what they have done about it, they almost always respond with "nothing I can do."

Most will claim that they exercise their opinions at the polls during elections, but this action will not influence the media or give them an accurate barometer of what the average citizen believes. Use the electronic advances to contact these news agencies and register complaints and praises to let the media leaders know how you feel. Too often we believe "polls" provide them with this feedback. The problem there is the way the polls are conducted. How big was the sample, was it spread across diverse groups, was it geographically focused? Skilled pollsters can ensure an outcome by carefully selecting how the poll was taken. It is the responsibility of the average citizen to make their opinions known and not depend on others to do it for them. Write, e-mail, tweet, call your media outlets when you are satisfied or not, and you will be surprised at the result, but only if a much larger segment of our society participates in this strategy. If you claim to not have the time, don't know who to contact, or the energy to make your voice heard, you are part of the problem. I am not suggesting that everyone should be a full-time activist; however, spending an hour a month providing input to your preferred media outlet is a civic duty that should not be ignored.

Despite examples above and the negative viewpoints regarding the news media in recent years, I believe a balanced news reporting process is a vital key to freedom and the advancement of a civilized world. I would challenge all news outlets to return to presenting facts versus opinions and aggressively report on the accuracy of the reporting. Many times the media and their "experts" miss the mark, but these failures are not reported as they feel it would negatively impact their credibility when nothing could be further from the truth. The admission of mistakes and/or corrections in position based on data collected would only lift people's opinion of news outlets.

Experts/Critics

In today's media, political, and corporate environment, the use of experts to express opinions, predict future events, and evaluate current and past events has become very widespread. This practice is not new as numerous examples can be found throughout history. With the development of digital communication and the tremendous growth of outlets for this type of analysis, the number of "experts" has risen significantly. I support the use of experts as a valuable source of data to assist in the analysis of any topic of the day whether it is political, scientific, social, or sports related. The data provided by these experts generally has the benefit of inside knowledge of the topic and as such must be weighed accordingly by those using the data to formulate their own opinions. The problem with this evaluation process is too many people act as if these experts are infallible and their conclusions are correct, especially if they support the position you advocate.

There are several problems with depending on experts to decide your position on any topic. What if the experts are wrong? If you believe there is a very low probability of this fact, look at the examples listed later in this chapter. Understand, by definition, that these experts are being asked to express an opinion based on their experiences in their respective fields. Like all opinions they are sometimes right and sometimes wrong. One would expect them to be correct more often due to their knowledge and experience; however, many times the issue they are evaluating has too many variables to reach an easy conclusion.

Take meteorologists as an example. Because of their training and experience, they are much more likely to provide the correct forecast versus the average person, but they do sometimes miss spectacularly. The average person, in this case, does understand that no one can accurately forecast the weather and be correct 100 percent of the time, so their misses are understood and accepted. Is this same standard applied to experts in other fields? It should be; they are expressing opinions in their related fields as well and should not be expected to be 100 percent correct. The other issue with experts is you can find these "experts" on both sides of the same issue. If either side were truly "experts" on any subject, they would agree on the same position because in most cases it would be clearly based on evidence at hand. This points to the real question, "What is an expert?"

Experts are individuals with training and/or experience in a specific field to enable them to develop a calculated opinion on a given topic. Nothing about that definition guarantees that this opinion will be correct. In my opinion experts are asked their views on a topic before the event happens, and those who comment afterward are known as critics. I will address the role of critics later in this chapter.

How are experts judged and evaluated? Who designates them as experts? How much weight should I place on the opinions of so-called experts? These are valid questions, and you must ask yourself how much you value their opinion. Let's say that we have two experts giving advice on the same subject from different sides of the issue. The topic is the effects of PTSD on individuals who have experienced a traumatic event. One expert is a professor who has researched and written several articles on the subject and the other is a doctor who has treated military personnel suffering from PTSD for fifteen years. Who do you believe has the most credibility? Neither is infallible, but you might want to lean slightly toward the opinion of the doctor with the hands-on experience. This does not mean that the professor does not have a different insight that is correct on aspects of the subject either. The fact that individuals are designated as "experts" should also be challenged. Would you believe the conclusions of an expert panel that claims motorcycles should be banned due to their perceived unsafe status if you found out that this panel of "experts" were staffed and funded by a group whose agenda was to outlaw motorcycles? This scenario plays out way too frequently in today's society.

The use of so-called experts to further an agenda with half-truths and in some cases false data has become widespread and makes it more difficult for the average person to get a clear picture of the situation. When evaluating the opinions of experts, you must first analyze their ability to be unbiased. Would you believe all data provided by a group named "Trump is our President" without balancing that opinion with views from the other side of the political spectrum? The opinions of "experts" must be compared to other relevant data sources to help anyone formulate their own opinions. The key point for every individual is to be confident that the opinion you formulate is as valid as any other opinion from any source. Those in government would like you to believe that they know more about the subjects and understand what is best for you and the rest of the population. Nothing could be further from the truth on most topics as they are isolated from the daily routines and challenges of the average person. I would admit that some issues regarding the military and foreign policy could be the exception as those in certain roles will be privy to confidential information that is not available to the population in general.

In order to become your own "expert," you will need to invest a little time. The advent of the digital age has provided a greater opportunity for the average person to do this than at any other time in history. When researching issues, specifically look for data that supports both sides of the issue you are researching. Try to place yourself on both sides of the issue to get a clear picture of both viewpoints. Self-discipline is important here as it is easy to believe data that supports your position and more difficult to give the same credence to data that supports the other side of the issue. You will know when you have been successful in this process when your research causes you to change your position on a given issue.

What happens when the experts are wrong? We all agree that they can't possibly be right 100 percent of the time, yet we rarely hear an "expert" admit that they were wrong. If these experts were to admit errors when they are discovered, they would have much more credibility. I would be remiss if I did not point out that some experts do retract previous opinions, and they certainly improve their standing with me as a result. I mentioned in the media chapter the position of *The Washington Post* on the name "Redskins" and their finding that the name was not nearly as offensive in the Native American community as had been reported. It took great integrity for the Post to report, based on research data, that their previous position was incorrect.

"The number of critics multiplies once the results are in." Critics are different than "experts" in that they are evaluating a topic that has already developed or played out. They criticize the experts or individuals that had to make decisions or take actions without the benefit of hindsight. I must note that a significant number of the "critics" are also "experts." They usually become critics of experts that were representing the other side of a given topic. This is not to say that we shouldn't critique events and issues after they have played out to learn from the experience. This process is vital to progress in any arena. The problem in reporting today is the proliferation of critics that are not qualified to critique the issue at hand. Celebrities with no experience critiquing politicians, law enforcement, and the military; nonmilitary critics outlining how the military should be run; people who have never had to deal with life or death situations describing what they feel should have been done in these situations; armchair athletes who never played organized sports. Any idiot can be a critic, the intelligent ones stand out.

There are examples of critics whose opinions were changed by presentation of facts. One that sticks out in my mind is Rev. Jarrett Maupin, a leader of protests regarding police use of force. His position regarding unnecessary use of force by law enforcement did not change (nor should it), but he did get a greater understanding of the situations facing law enforcement personnel by taking a training course offered by the Maricopa County Sheriff's Office in Phoenix, Arizona. In the training scenarios, he was killed, then killed a suspect, and finally resolved the last without shots fired. After the training, he said that he would change his message to his followers and tell them that compliance with police orders is imperative to reducing the use of deadly force by law enforcement and keeping both parties safe. Any violations of police protocols could be addressed after the interaction through proper channels. Rev. Maupin is not the only one to have this experience as several others have gone through a similar deadly force training program with similar results. This fact does not suggest that the use of deadly force has always been justified. There are numerous cases where deadly force should not have been used and those officers must be held accountable for their actions.

Let's look at some historical examples of experts/critics' opinions that turned out to be woefully incorrect. Don't overlook the fact that these individuals were, in fact, brilliant and/or extremely talented and certainly had many opinions or predictions that were right on point.

- "Heavier than air flying machines are impossible."—Lord Kelvin, President of the Royal Society, 1895. He was proven wrong in eight years.
- "Sensible and responsible women do not want to vote."—Grover Cleveland, 1905. Imagine this comment today!
- "Everything that can be invented has been invented."—Charles H. Duell, Director of the US Patent Office, 1899
- "Babe Ruth made a big mistake when he gave up pitching."—Tris Speaker, 1921. Speaker is in the MLB Hall of Fame.
- "There is no likelihood that man can ever tap the power of the atom."—Robert Millikan, Nobel Prize winner for Physics, 1923
- "Stocks have reached what looks like a permanently high plateau."—Irving Fisher, Professor of Economics, Yale University, 1929. Weeks later the market would crash, triggering the Great Depression, and stock prices would not reach those levels again for twenty-five years.
- "Man will never reach the moon regardless of all future scientific advances."—Dr. Lee de Forest, Father of Radio and Voice on Film
- "The bomb will never go off. I speak as an expert in explosives."—Admiral William Leahy on the US Atomic Bomb Project

- "I think there is a world market for maybe five computers."—Thomas Watson, Chairman of IBM, 1943. His shareholders are sure glad he was wrong!
- "We don't like their sound, and guitar music is on its way out."—Decca Recording Co. rejecting the Beatles, 1962

How about this string of predictions from Earth Day 1970?

- Civilization will end within fifteen to thirty years unless immediate action is taken against problems facing mankind.—Harvard Biologist George Wald
- Population will inevitably and completely outstrip whatever small increases in food supplies we make. At least one hundred to two hundred million people per year will be starving to death during the next ten years.—Stanford Biologist Paul Ehrlich (He also predicted hundreds of thousands would die in the next few years of air pollution.)
- One theory assumes that the earth's cloud cover will continue to thicken as more pollutants, water vapor, and dust are belched into the atmosphere by industrial smokestacks and jet airplanes. Screened from the sun's heat, the planet will cool, and a new ice age will begin.—*Newsweek* magazine
- By the year 2000, if present trends continue, we are using crude oil at such a rate that there won't be any more crude oil.—Ecologist Kenneth Watt (who also predicted the new ice age beginning in 1990)
- The north polar ice cap will be free of ice within five years."—Al Gore, 2009 (In November 2017, ice growth was at a rate of 30,900 square miles per day.)
- Barack Obama will never be president.—Charles Krauthammer, Mark Penn, Rush Limbaugh, William Kristol, Jeffrey Kuhner
- Donald Trump will never be president.—Barack Obama, Stephen Colbert, John Oliver, Bill Maher, Nate Silver

- A Trump Presidency will trigger a worldwide recession.—Paul Krugman, Economist, *New York Times*. The economy has seen significant growth since Trump's election, setting new records in reduced unemployment, stock market gains, and tax reductions.

The proliferation of these experts and critics has had a significant effect on the negative outlook of the population in general. Nearly all experts and critics push doom and gloom for the future. Why is this happening? First, doom and gloom sell. Creating fear among people is a way to generate interest and the subsequent revenue generation through book sales, television ratings, and personal appearances by the experts and critics. Since they are rarely, if ever, called to the carpet to explain their mistakes, there is no downside for reckless and inaccurate predictions. Paul Krugman, mentioned above, is known as the "Lord of Wrong Predictions" as up to half of his predictions are wrong. He also blamed Trump for an outbreak of cholera in Puerto Rico after a recent hurricane disaster. The CDC reported that cholera was not found in Puerto Rico. Why does the *New York Times* keep his byline? Because the controversy he generates sells papers.

The existence of experts and critics are vital to forward progress in any society. They perform a vital link in our freedoms because they are free to speak their minds (that pesky First Amendment again). Since the media outlets will not judge their accuracy and/or print acknowledgments of their failures, we must take it upon ourselves to analyze and evaluate their predictions and criticisms. Despite the negativity produced by these individuals, life in general is very good for the overwhelming majority of citizens. Things can always be better, but that does not mean they are bad.

In closing remember that at one point in history the most brilliant experts on the planet Earth believed that the Earth was flat!

Politically Correct

How can an idea that sounds so good turn out so negative? The concept of political correctness is very comfortable. Who doesn't think that people should be considerate in their actions and words to prevent others from embarrassment, ridicule, and being emotionally offended? We all agree that we do not want to unintentionally offend people. Trying to phrase speech, restrict actions, and eliminate labels to meet this end sounds like a very worthwhile endeavor. So why has this spun completely out of control to the point where the idea itself has become somewhat of a joke and is generally regarded as a veiled effort to ignore reality?

One of the primary problems with political correctness is the premise that you can reach a state where no one is offended. This is an impossible goal to attain as every position an individual can take on any subject will have more than one viewpoint. Any position taken has the potential and likelihood that it will offend someone. This creates an additional problem. What is or isn't politically correct? The answer to this question varies by individual. Certainly we can all agree that using racial slurs, laughing at disabilities, and making light of struggles by individuals or groups should be ostracized by the public in general. Have we gone too far with this idea as to create an environment where everything is taken far too seriously? It seems that every comment is now deemed to offend someone. What happens when someone is offended? *Nothing!* The right to not be offended does not exist. If you are offended by a TV show or movie, turn it off. If certain types of music offend you, don't listen. If a political party offends you, support the opposition.

The term "politically correct" was first used in 1793 in a United States Supreme Court judgment on a political issue. It was used sporadically during the 1800s in the United States and other English-speaking countries. In the early 1900s, communists and socialists used it to define adherence to a particular doctrine. Their message is that there is only one correct position on any subject, theirs. Opposing viewpoints were considered politically incorrect and subjected those who held these views to oppression by their own governments. In 1934, the Nazis limited reporting to only pure Aryans who were said to be politically correct. In Nazi Germany, any who opposed the "politically correct" doctrine of the Nazi Party were removed to labor camps or worse. Similar actions were taken in the Soviet Union, China, and other oppressive regimes although the term itself was not used in those countries. The strategy in these regimes included shouting down opposition without ever considering the opposing viewpoints, discrimination against those who held opposing views, the elimination of free debate on topics, and ultimately imprisoning and/or killing those who held opposing viewpoints.

Clearly political correctness does not promote freedom and respect for those who hold different views. In the current United States political scene, both parties attempt to use this strategy to support their own political agendas. Republicans and Democrats claim to be inclusive but using political correctness to further an agenda broadens division as neither side promotes tolerance of the other.

Political correctness can also be used to soften the blow of certain realities. Ask anyone in America and they will tell you that slavery has been eliminated in our country. Yet these same people will admit that human trafficking is a problem. Human trafficking is slavery! It occurs in nearly every country in the world and is not limited by race, religion, or national origin. In some countries it is still a legal practice. Doesn't the term "human trafficking" sound so much better than "slavery"? Sounds more like moving people around rather than keeping them captive and forcing them into labor or the sex trade. People caught in this trap are beaten, sexually abused, tortured, bought and sold, and even killed. This is no different than slaves in the American south before 1864.

In the name of political correctness, terms have been changed to try and create a more accepting viewpoint. Queer changed to gay, retarded changed to special needs, handicapped changed to physically challenged are all examples, and I can say that these changes were positive as they reflect the changing views of society in general. By distancing ourselves from hurtful phrases and tags from the past, political correctness can have positive results.

The problem comes from the extreme examples where the claim that someone may be offended drives actions not supported by the majority of society. One of the early examples was the Frito Bandito cartoon character used to promote Fritos corn chips from 1967 to 1971. The first iteration of this character included a scruffy beard, messy hair, and a gold tooth and was deemed to be demeaning by the National Mexican American Anti-Defamation Committee. The character was changed to be clean shaven, lost the gold tooth, and had neatly combed hair. Still in 1971, Frito-Lay decided to retire the character because they still received some negative feedback. My closest friend at that time was Mexican American, and he was very disappointed as he liked the character. This is not to say that the campaign wasn't canceled solely because it had run its course or that the company felt it may have been impacting sales. My only point here was that not all Mexican Americans found him offensive. It seems that any caricature today is deemed offensive.

Does that mean that the comic strip *Beetle Baily* is offensive to white Americans because he is lazy and always trying to get out of work? I don't believe that to be the case. Another case would have been a Snickers commercial in 1990 where a football player takes a hard hit on the field and when asked who he was, he responded, "I am Batman." The commercial was very funny but pulled because it made light of concussions and was deemed offensive to those suffering from brain injuries. That commercial did not make anyone doubt the seriousness of brain injuries.

We are also seeing political correctness used to reevaluate historical events. Some of our founding fathers are now being vilified by some because they owned slaves. Let's be clear, slavery was legal at that time. It certainly was an abomination then as it is now, but it was legal. Interestingly enough the same founding fathers wrote a constitution that would lead to the downfall of slavery in the United

States in less than one hundred years. Trying to demean the accomplishments of the founders of our nation by applying the moral code of today on the history of the past is absurd.

Another recent trend is the removal of monuments and statues from the Civil War era as offensive to black Americans. In all my years on this planet, I have not heard this issue from any of my black friends. Charles Barkley, NBA Hall of Fame player, said that he never once thought about those statues in his life. I wonder how they can be offensive since they represent the losing side in the Civil War. Instead they should be viewed as reminders that promoting an oppressive agenda that included slavery will never succeed in America. I do support the right of individual communities to make decisions based on the wishes of the local citizenry. If the majority of those in the community wish to remove these monuments, they certainly have that right. That would apply to any monuments and statues, not just those representing the Civil War leaders from the Confederate states.

The application of political correctness with potentially dangerous consequences is in the United States military. I am a Marine, and I fully support the entrance of women into combat roles. They can and do fly fighter jets, combat helicopters, crew on navy ships, and many other combat roles. In these roles they have proven that they can meet the same standards as their male counterparts. They have received medals for bravery in combat and should receive the same level of respect and admiration as their male counterparts. I do not believe that they should be placed in ground infantry units due to the physical differences between male and female troops. The Marine Corps ran tests in war games with a fully male unit versus a unit integrated with women. The results were as expected. The all-male unit outperformed the integrated unit. This test was not taken lightly as the Marine Corps trained three hundred male and one hundred female Marines together for a year prior to the test to ensure a fair evaluation.

The all-male unit outperformed the gender-integrated unit on 69 percent of the 134 tasks measured during the exercise. In every case during field movements, the male unit was faster; on marksmanship the males hit their targets 44 percent of the time versus 28 percent for the females, and injuries for women were 40 percent versus 19 percent for the males. In addition the women participants had difficulty negotiating vertical obstacles due to difference in upper body strength. Please don't overlook the fact that these are some bad-ass women who have trained hard for this role. The average male in this study was 178 pounds with 20 percent body fat, and the women were 142 pounds with 24 percent body fat. This study was set up to ensure the result was honest and unbiased. This study did not address one aspect of combat that doesn't often occur in today's warfare, hand-to-hand combat.

Despite all the examples in Hollywood of 130 pound women taking down 200 pound men, it does not reflect reality. A good argument could be made that 130 pound men don't do so well against 200 pound men either, and that would be a correct statement, but they do better than 130 pound women. To test this theory, why don't middleweight female UFC fighters compete with middleweight male UFC fighters? That answer is obvious. There will be those that say the gender-integrated unit can still win on the field of battle. While this may be true, how many additional casualties (male and female) are you willing to sacrifice due to slower movements, poorer marksmanship, difficulty negotiating obstacles, and a higher rate of injury? Some will say that it's acceptable to achieve equality, but only those who don't have military-service-age children.

I don't believe that one American life should be sacrificed on an altar of political correctness. To keep this in the proper perspective, of the two million jobs in the United States military, only 220,000 (11 percent) are not open to women. The officers involved with the study also indicated that this issue should not be closed forever, that they would continue to evaluate the performance of women in these roles with the thought that additional training could improve some of the deficient performance. It should be noted that in the past year, two women completed the Army's Ranger School. If any woman can pass the same tests as their male counterparts with the same level of competency, I certainly would not deny them the opportunity to serve in that capacity.

On a similar note, twenty-nine women Marines attempted to pass the Marine Combat Officer training, and none passed. Remember this fact, the military is not a social experiment. Its sole purpose is to kill the enemy while staying alive to continue the fight. Their goal is "maximum combat effectiveness," and that can't be achieved at this time with gender-integrated infantry units. I will close this paragraph with a salute to women in the military who have demonstrated courage and valor equal to anyone in military service.

Political correctness has been proven over history to be a failed philosophy. Rather than improve society, it has contributed to some of the worst events in history. It flies directly in the face of freedom of speech and preaches a doctrine of a single ideology. The true path to freedom is the acceptance that opposing views can coexist and have respect for each other. Fortunately political correctness is viewed by a majority of the population as somewhat of a joke. Allowing our elected representatives to use this doctrine to pass laws and restrict our freedoms must be carefully monitored to prevent restrictions of our freedoms. Instead of worrying about being politically correct, why don't we try to be more courteous and understanding to all around us on a daily basis? This more positive approach will make everyone more comfortable and happier.

Sports

The sporting world has been through significant changes over the last fifty years. The attitude has changed from goals of good sportsmanship and competitive play to a mentality of win at all costs. This change has generated a negative view of all sports and their participants in the media and in many fan's view as well. I grew up in the 1950s and 1960s, in what some refer to as a golden age of sports. Baseball was the national pastime and was expanding to new markets. Football was gaining popularity at both the NFL and college level. Basketball was also gaining in popularity and was building a foundation for the significant explosion of interest in the 1970s and 1980s. Hockey also saw slow but steady growth in the fan base and media coverage during the period. During this period (1950s through 1980s) the drive to win at all costs began to erode the acceptance that everyone was a winner if they competed at the peak of their abilities.

When I was growing up, if your team finished the season with a winning record, they were said to have had a good season. Grantland Rice, legendary sports reporter of the early twentieth century (the first golden age of sports), stated, "It's not that you won or lost but how you played the game." There was honor and respect for those who lost but gave their all in the competition. You could be proud and hope that the next season or contest brought additional success. In today's sports environment, there is one winner (the champion) and all the rest are losers.

How did this happen? What drove this changed attitude? The simple answer would be to blame the money. The revenue generated by sports dramatically increased over the years. As the stakes increased, so did the emphasis on winning. The phrase "winning isn't everything, it's the only thing" was first quoted by Red Sanders, head football coach at UCLA in 1950. It has been mistakenly attributed to Vince Lombardi of NFL fame as he used the phrase on many occasions. Lombardi did change his view and stated that he wished he had never used the quote. It was this drive to win that caused a number of issues in sports to change.

The first sports to change were the professional ranks of the MLB, NFL, NBA, and NHL as the owners found that they had just tapped a growing revenue model driven largely by television and the ability to reach into homes miles away from their locations whose viewers would have little opportunity to physically attend the event. The broadcast networks saw the impact these sporting events had on ratings (which drove advertising revenue) and began to aggressively bid for broadcast rights, driving up the revenues for the leagues. The increasing revenues were also tied to winning as the best teams were featured on the "game of the week" that were nationally televised while those with average records only received local television revenues.

Imagine the imbalance of local television revenues between the New York Yankees and, say, the Baltimore Orioles. In 1960 New York City had a population of nearly eight million while Baltimore had a population of just over six hundred thousand. This guaranteed that New York would have a significant revenue advantage over a team that was expected to compete on the same level. Why didn't the Yankees win it all every year? Well they almost did in the 1950s and 1960s, but the saving grace for all MLB teams at that time was the "reserve clause" which forced a baseball player to only play for the team that drafted him unless he was traded. This clause allowed the owners to effectively control players and their compensation. During the 1960s some players began to exercise their power of negotiation via the only method available to them at the time, the holdout. Refusing to play unless certain monetary goals were met.

Sandy Koufax and Don Drysdale, Hall of Fame pitchers, refused to report to spring training in 1966 unless they received significant increases in compensation (they would become the first pitchers to earn more than $100,000/year). They held out for a month of spring training before the Los Angeles Dodgers relented and paid them.

The key here was if the Dodgers did not sign two of the best pitchers in baseball who had led them to a World Series title in 1965, they would be an average team at best in 1966. They returned to the World Series in that year. The rising revenue of the owners drove the players to want to share in the revenues. The "reserve clause" eliminated the leverage that the players felt would help them achieve their goal, and in 1970 Curt Flood, an all-star outfielder, filed a lawsuit against major league baseball challenging the clause. Although he didn't win the suit, the US Supreme Court stated that the reserve clause should be challenged in collective bargaining, and the players union was born.

By 1976 the collective bargaining resulted in "free agency," and the players had gotten the right to negotiate with any team once their current contracts expired. Owners and some members of the media indicated that this would have a negative impact on the sport and predicted doom for major league baseball. Instead it created a boom in the sport by allowing smaller market teams to compete for top players and created competitive balance. It should be noted that until baseball agreed to a luxury tax on payrolls above a certain limit, larger market teams continued to have a significant advantage.

The additional revenue began to change attitudes of the owners, players, fans, and the sports media as well, and the focus was narrowed to winning, not the competition. This phenomenon carried over into all sports, especially those televised nationally like the NFL, MLB, NBA, NHL, Olympics, major college sports, and other sports (golf, tennis, etc.). The change was gradual, but it continued in the opinions of the owners (very competitive individuals), the media, and eventually the fans. It was no longer acceptable to finish with a winning record, win your division, or even play for the championship unless you won. The Atlanta Falcons had a great year in 2016 losing the Super Bowl to the New England Patriots in what many describe as the greatest Super Bowl ever played. If you asked fans in Atlanta, even weeks after the game, what they thought, many would have referred to them as the same old losers.

Players, who have always earned more than the average American, now earn riches beyond belief to play games. This caused a disconnect with the fans when players make remarks, like Latrell Sprewell who claimed that he needed more than the $30 million offered by the Minnesota Timberwolves to "feed his family." To the average fan, this was an outrage as they managed to feed their family on significantly less than $30 million. I don't begrudge the athletes for the compensation they receive. They are entitled to a significant salary based on the total revenues generated. Most professional athletes are extremely grateful for the opportunities that their physical ability has given them, and many give back to their communities. It is the few that, like Sprewell, make statements or take actions that indicate a lack of appreciation for their situation that generate ill will from the fan base. I would be remiss if I didn't point out that if I had been given $20 million dollars at age twenty-two and was constantly surrounded by those praising me, I would likely have been a big jerk. Don't forget that these young athletes have not reached a point of mental maturity, in some cases, to appreciate their good fortune.

The owners, often referred to as the "billionaire boys club," have driven the cost of attending a sporting event to the point that the average citizen can't afford to take their family to games on any regular basis. Their drive to constantly find ways to increase revenues has caused many fans to develop negative opinions of professional sports. They push local governments to fund arenas with the promise of increased revenues that never seem to materialize. They create luxury boxes that only the incredibly rich can afford (and use access to these boxes by politicos as incentive to support the new arena), drive up ticket prices for season packages, charge outrageous prices for concessions, souvenirs, and parking without considering the impact on average Americans or their ability to attend. Their position is that as long as they have those who will pay the price, who cares about the average American. This mentality, I call "short-term profit myopia," will have a negative long-term impact on major professional sports.

The inability of families to frequently go to games diminishes the importance of the sport to younger fans. The result is that they don't follow these franchises like their parents. I was a huge fan of MLB, NFL, and the NBA. Neither of my children follow any team from those professional leagues, despite my best efforts to draw them in. Recent television ratings in all sports have been down on average. Don't be fooled by those who explain these numbers away as anomalies due to certain economic or political events, and don't misunderstand my position. Major sports are not going away, the professional leagues will survive although the popularity of these sports as a percentage of the population is declining. In a recent airing of the game show *Jeopardy*, a category on the NFL did not solicit a single correct response from the three players. None even attempted to answer. To keep perspective, I answered each question easily.

College sports are no exception. The drive to win in an environment of insane revenues in primarily two sports, football and basketball, has caused athletes to be exploited, cheating by college officials and alumni, and a general disregard of the purpose of college athletics. The players are supposed to be scholar athletes who attend the college to further their education and prepare for life. Many college athletes fit this description to a tee as there are numerous college sports that don't drive revenues, and those athletes play for the love of the game and to get an education. My daughter played soccer at a NCAA DII school and had a wonderful experience.

Let's look into some realities of college athletics. The major DI schools maintain that the revenue generated by the two major sports are needed to support the lesser sports (especially those for women), and without this revenue they could not stay in compliance with Title IX that dictates equal opportunities for female athletes. I would ask them to explain how all the DII, DIII, and NAIA schools manage to stay in compliance without the riches of the NCAA Division I schools. Athletes such as Dexter Manley who made it through four years at Oklahoma State despite being functionally illiterate are a prime example of the exploitation of key athletes (realizing that athletes not deemed necessary to win are not exploited in this fashion). Long as you could produce on the field, you could get by with the help of teachers and school administrators looking the other way. The fact that Dexter is a very likable individual certainly helped. Since those days the NCAA has made it much more difficult for this situation to exist, but cheaters are still identified each year.

The lure of the money does not only apply to the owners and college administrators but to the athletes themselves before and after turning professional. The use of steroids to boost performance and help land that scholarship or next big contract is rampant despite steps taken by colleges and professional leagues to curb their use. This usage has caused many former fans to turn their backs on the sports they used to love. Complicating the issue is the insistence by some in the media that cheating should not disqualify the cheater from awards and inclusion into the Hall of Fame in their respective sport. Major league baseball is one of the most hypocritical leagues in this example. Much discussion on the inclusion into the Hall of Fame of players such as Barry Bonds, Mark McGwire, Rafael Palmeiro, and others who put up Hall of Fame worthy numbers is ridiculous considering that Shoeless Joe Jackson was banned for life for the "Black Sox" scandal in the 1919 World Series. This, despite the fact he batted .375 in the Series, handled thirty chances in the outfield without an error, hit the only home run of the series, and set a record with twelve hits in the series that was not broken until 1964.

Another example is Pete Rose, the career leader in hits who was banned by Commissioner Bart Giamatti. Although it was proven that Pete bet on ball games as a player coach in 1985 through 1987, he never bet against his team and was never accused of trying to impact the outcome of a game. If baseball wants to allow those proven or implicated with substantial evidence to have used steroids, then they must lift the ban on Shoeless Joe and Pete. I really do not blame the athletes since many of us would have taken that path if it meant millions of dollars. The owners of the teams certainly weren't overly concerned until it became journalistic topic. It's hard not to notice a 150 pound second baseman turning into a 190 pound outfielder in a year and suddenly hitting thirty home runs.

In spite of the negative views and attitudes referenced above, sports are a very positive influence in society. Many professional athletes give back to their communities through charitable foundations, personal involvement, and personal contributions. In the aftermath of Hurricane Harvey devastation in Houston, JJ Watt and Deshaun Watson made huge contributions to the recovery in that city. Others such as Peyton Manning, Dikembe Mutombo, Serena Williams, LeBron James, Tom Brady, David Beckham, and hundreds of others have generated hundreds of millions in charitable contributions. In addition to money, many athletes have personally visited hospitals to meet with sick children, held camps for disadvantaged youths, and sponsored youth athletic leagues. Can you imagine the joy a sick child must feel when visited by one of their athletic heroes?

Many college athletes contribute through personal appearances since they don't have the financial resources of the professionals. College athletics provide school pride, healthy activity for students who participate and attend games, and opportunities to attend college for some who otherwise would not be able due to financial constraints. The most important aspect of sports lies in the youth leagues all over America in all sports. In these leagues young people learn to enjoy success, handle adversity, contribute to a team, respect their competition, and learn the benefit of hard work to improve. I personally coached youth sports for over fifteen years, and it was more rewarding than all of my participation or following professional or college sports. The fact that I had numerous parents thank me for the positive influence I had on their children was worth a lot more than money. I was a good coach, and my teams typically won more games than they lost, but the focus wasn't on winning, it was on doing your best and feeling good about that fact. Although there are some examples of poor youth coaching as a result of the "winning is everything" attitude and some who try to live vicariously through their children, they are a very small minority, and I must salute and praise the thousands of youth coaches nationwide who provide the true meaning of sports to the young people in their charge.

Celebrities

There are few groups that generate more negative feelings in today's society than celebrities (politicians would be one, more on that later). These opinions are sometimes well deserved but, in many instances, are overstated. Celebrities are defined as those who have come to be known by a significant segment of society. It would include actors/actresses, talk show hosts, columnists, athletes, and any others who have gained national recognition due to events and/or exposure to national media. The impact of the digital age and its multitude of outlets has provided celebrities with a much greater opportunity to get their thoughts and opinions in front of the population in general. These thoughts and opinions are sometimes well received and at other times vilified by the population.

The lack of accountability by those reporting these opinions often leads to these celebrities being misquoted, comments taken out of context, and some that are actual fabrications. Unfortunately, in many cases, the opinions have been accurately reported and demonstrate how removed from daily life many of these celebrities have become despite their personal history. The problem is not the fact that celebrities make their opinions known as I fully support their right to speak their minds on any subject they chose. It is the importance that some people and some in the media seem to place on their opinions. The celebrities themselves in some cases have developed an overstated impression of the impact of their comments. They sometimes mistakenly believe that they are making a "difference" in society with their comments. The reality is that their opinions are no more valid than any citizen. I would agree that some of their opinions have brought to light issues of importance and have generated activity that does make a "difference."

Let's look at some examples where the opinions and, more importantly, the actions of celebrities have indeed made a difference. During World War II, many celebrities supported America's war effort by encouraging people to buy war bonds, support rationing, making films to bolster morale among the troops and population. In stark contrast to today, many volunteered for service although I would say the circumstances in 1941 are different than those of today. Some such as former NFL player Pat Tillman made the ultimate sacrifice in the service of his country as recently as 2004. Other celebrities that have made this sacrifice include Glenn Miller, band leader (WWII); Leslie Howard, actor in *Gone with the Wind* (WWII); Hobie Baker, hockey (WWI); Jake Lummus, football (WWII, Medal of Honor); Bob Kalsu, football (Vietnam); and Cathy Wayne, Australian singer (Vietnam). Multitudes of celebrities have spent time in war zones to entertain the troops. Bob Hope symbolized this commitment that is still in play today with many celebrities continuing the tradition he began during the 1940s.

The civil rights movement is another example of celebrities making a difference. Many did more than express their opinions as they got involved on a personal level.

Celebrities such as the following:

- Harry Belafonte
- Ossie Davis
- Ruby Dee
- Sammy Davis Jr.
- Sidney Poitier
- Marlon Brando
- Charlton Heston
- Burt Lancaster
- Jackie Robinson
- Muhammed Ali
- Bill Russell
- Jim Brown
- Paul Newman
- Elizabeth Taylor
- Kareem Abdul Jabbar

And many others were directly involved through actions that could have had a negative impact on their careers. There is no doubt that their involvement helped to speed the process of racial equality and the signing of the Civil Rights Act of 1964. This attitude of action was also demonstrated by Al Davis, owner of the Oakland Raiders, who in 1963 refused to play a game in Mobile, Alabama, because of the segregation laws in place at the time. He also refused to play in any city that would not allow all his players to stay in the same hotel. This type of commitment was not only present in the USA. In 1995, Francois Pienaar, a white South African player on the National Rugby Team, formed an alliance with Nelson Mandela, newly elected President of South Africa. The nation was going through many changes, and one topic was the use of the springbok as a national symbol as it has been used by the former Apartheid government. Nelson Mandela was vocal in his support of the South African National Rugby Team and wore a hat and shirt supporting them, springbok proudly displayed. The leadership displayed by these two helped to strengthen the unity of the nation. The fact that the national team, the Springboks, won the Rugby World Cup that year only enhanced the impact.

Celebrity involvement in charitable causes is literally off the chart. Hundreds of millions of dollars have been raised, much of it through personal contribution. Oprah Winfrey alone has raised over one hundred million dollars. These charities receive support from multiple celebrities, UNICEF, Red Cross, Make-A-Wish, St. Jude, Habitat for Humanity, and many, many others. Some celebrities have their own foundations/charitable organizations that address specific needs around the globe. They address education, eradication of disease, clean water, food supplies, help for refugees, and the list goes on and on.

A listing of just a few of these celebrities and their contributions would include the following:

- Oprah Winfrey—over $100 million
- Jami Gertz/Anthony Ressler—$10,569,000 (2010)
- Herb Alpert—$9,104,829 (2010)

- Mel Gibson—$6,853,020 (2010)
- Ndamukong Suh, NFL player—$2,600,000 (2010)
- Lance Berkman, MLB player—$2,412,245 (2010)

Many others such as Alicia Keys, Taylor Swift, Kevin Durant, Carrie Underwood, Gary Sinise, Dikembe Mutombo, Elton John, Justin Bieber, Ellen DeGeneres, Willie Nelson, and many others, way too many to list here, are significant contributors to worthwhile charities and causes. Forbes reported that 2,258 charitable causes are supported by celebrities. Imagine the impact of these donations worldwide. Imagine the impact if these individuals were not involved!

These facts would lead us to ask, "How did celebrities come to be perceived in such a negative light?" Several factors are involved. The media focus on their more controversial comments and actions, outrageous behavior, the hypocrisy of some regarding social/political issues, and a lack of understanding of the challenges of everyday life for the vast majority not blessed with the riches that celebrity can generate. The percentage of celebrities that participate or support the kind of behaviors that would generate this negative publicity and public perception is small. Unfortunately, some are very well-known and as a result get plenty of media coverage.

In my opinion the hypocrisy of some celebrities is what drives a lot of the negative views held by the general public. Take gun control as an example. Many celebrities have come out on gun control, but a surprisingly small number support a ban on guns even though public opinion seems to think all celebrities want guns banned. In fact some have been vocal supporters of gun rights, and they are not all from the same side of the political spectrum.

Those who support banning guns are as follows:

- Sylvester Stallone's movies glorify gun violence. He Supports house-to-house confiscation.
- Mark Wahlberg would love to have them taken away.
- Rosie O'Donnell, "People who own guns should be put in jail."
- Michael Moore

The interesting fact is these individuals are protected by armed security personnel.

Those who support reasonable gun control measures are as follows:

- Snoop Dogg
- Britney Spears
- Alyssa Milano
- Stephen King

These individuals advocate steps that would improve screening to acquire guns and restrictions that would take guns out of the hands of those who may not be responsible owners.

Those who support gun rights are as follows:

- Brad Pitt
- Eva Longoria
- Tom Selleck
- Gary Sinise
- Angelina Jolie

These individuals may also support reasonable improvements to existing gun control laws.

The one fact I would like to highlight is that celebrities are no different than the average citizens on the topic of gun control. They have differing opinions and can't be lumped into a single group. I have only identified a few in each category for perspective.

Another example of hypocrisy by celebrities is the recent sexual harassment revelations highlighted by charges against Harvey Weinstein. Over a period of thirty years, he is accused of harassing, coercing, or raping over eighty women in the entertainment industry. Because of his significant influence in the industry, he was allowed to continue this behavior even though his actions were common knowledge. Entertainers such as Gwyneth Paltrow alluded to this fact as early as 1998 on David Letterman's show. Courtney Love advised young actresses, "If Harvey invites you to a private party at the Four Seasons, don't go."

Many of the people now claiming to be appalled at these revelations have been shown to have praised him for his role in Hollywood, had pictures taken with him, and benefitted from their association. Some political candidates accepted donations from him even though they were advised of the allegations against him. The backlash from the charges against Weinstein has caused other influential men in Hollywood to have their past actions brought to light. The names are well-known and include several who have already resigned positions, been terminated, or are facing legal action. I have heard someone asked, "How many of these accusers complied to further their careers?" That question is completely irrelevant. It is the act of using one's position and power over the success or failure of another that is the problem. Hollywood further creates hypocrisy by claiming that the problem is equally pervasive throughout all of society. Statistical data does not support that position although complaints have seen an increase nationwide. It is a problem in all of society but not as prevalent as shown in Hollywood. We can only hope that the #MeToo movement and other efforts will help eliminate this boorish and illegal behavior. The elimination of the "casting couch" mentality, long a tongue in cheek fact, is drastically overdue.

Hollywood celebrities are not the only celebrities accused of this behavior as politicians from Clarence Thomas to Al Franken have been accused along with others. Business leaders are not immune either, but with the mandates by corporations to provide sexual harassment training and processes to report offenders, it has become more difficult for executives or other employees to engage in this behavior without immediate consequences.

What happened to all the celebrities who were going to "leave the country" if a specific law was passed, a specific individual was elected, or due to some other social issue? The list is extensive and not restricted to a single topic or election. It has been reported that Chelsea Handler, Neve Campbell, Al Sharpton, Samuel L. Jackson, George Lopez, Barbra Streisand, Whoopi Goldberg, Miley Cyrus, Ruth Bader Ginsburg, Amy Schumer all made these statements and yet are still here. I did not add names of those who said they would move to Jupiter, another planet, etc. as I view these as rhetoric, not a promise to leave. Do they think the average American cares? Most would help them pack. They also threatened to not make movies, TV shows, or appear on stage. Again do you think Americans care? Entertainers and athletes sometimes think they are irreplaceable. Think about this, in twenty years, you will be as popular as those twenty years ago are today. Entertainers and athletes vanish from the public's view all the time and are rarely missed even if it is noticed. There will always be those who are standing by to take your place.

I believe most prevalent reason the public has taken a negative view toward celebrities is the outrageous comments and acts. These actions seem to generate the greatest coverage, mostly through social media, and tend to stay in the spotlight longer. One of the most notorious acts was committed by Kathy Griffin when she posted a picture of her holding a bloody head of President Donald Trump. This action generated extreme public outrage, and the backlash against her was immediate and severe. She has since stated that her career is now over because of this backlash. No kidding. What did she expect the reaction to be? Frankly she was lucky she wasn't arrested as her action could easily have been interpreted as a threat on the president's life. Fortunately cooler heads prevailed, and her actions were viewed as a weak attempt to get her name in the news.

The public comments by a few celebrities criticizing political figures, public policies, and military actions create another vehicle for public opinion to decline. Some celebrities seem to believe that wealth, fame, and/or the athletic skill bring intelligence. High school dropouts like Cher calling a president who graduated from Yale an idiot is a perfect example. LeBron James believes he is "too important to society" to not state his political views. Although I support his right to state his political views, he is way off base about his importance to society. The vast majority of Americans could not care less about LeBron. Just what is it that makes him believe he is important to society? He should take note of other "important" athletes from the past who are no longer relevant. In a few years when his playing days are over, the spotlight will vanish. Not long after that young people in general will not know who you were. Money does not make anyone smart or give them wisdom. It does in some cases give them a forum to express their personal opinions not available to the average citizen.

One of the most interesting things regarding these actions is the disbelief by these celebrities that they have a financial consequence. They somehow believe that they can say or do things that turn off their fans but that these same fans will continue to buy their records, see their movies, or buy tickets to their sporting events. The NFL discovered, in a large way, the impact on revenues caused by behavior offensive to many fans. The protests of the national anthem did not generate support for the very worthy cause of eliminating unnecessary use of deadly force by police. I would argue that it deflected attention from the cause and had little impact, if any, on changes. What if these players, in conjunction with the NFLPA, had designed a strategy to address this problem that would generate actual results. Forming focus groups with community leaders and law enforcement to address the real problems causing this issue and putting plans in place to improve the trust between the community and law enforcement, identify those who abuse their position and remove them from service, and cooperate with each other to reduce crime and its impact in the community. Identifying key players to act as spokesmen for the cause and developing a platform that generated change (see the actions of key athletes during the civil rights movement), creating a protest before or after the game such as meeting at midfield and kneeling in prayer or locking arms in solidarity would all have been received as positive actions to address a real problem. Insulting the country that allows you to become very wealthy by playing a game is not going to generate support. Interestingly some players participating in these protests when questioned on what they were protesting gave differing answers.

I don't believe that viewing all celebrities in a negative light based on the actions of a few is justified. When reviewing the overall impact of the entertainment, media, and sports industries, it is apparent that their overall contribution to society is very positive. Unfortunately, they seem to be their own worst enemy as they generate and report the negative publicity. The old adage that "All publicity is good publicity" has proven to be far from true. I have noticed that in many cases, some of the more outrageous actions and statements have come from celebrities no longer in the limelight or whose careers are in decline. Most of the celebrities at the peak of their careers avoid controversial topics, or if they respond, they do so in a respectful and well-thought-out response. I would also encourage celebrities to continue to be involved in social and political issues. They should remember this, protests do not change anything, actions change things. As noted at the beginning of this chapter, actions by celebrities have had a very positive impact on society, and I would encourage them to follow their example.

Politics

Politics is the single most divisive force in America today and rightfully so as it is the representation of the varying views on a wide range of subjects facing the citizens of the land. This does not mean that it must become the toxic, negative, rhetoric machine it has become over the last forty years. We no longer demand to know the position of our candidates on important issues as much as we indulge ourselves in character assassination that benefits only career politicians who are concerned with reelection and furthering their own personal wealth and prestige over the wishes of the American people. Both sides of the aisle claim that it is the other side preventing the progress that the American citizens expect while refusing to compromise with the other side to possibly reach an agreement that would satisfy a large majority.

These same politicians claim that they represent American values when the reality of the situation is that they are supposed to represent the views of their constituents. They pass laws that benefit themselves and bestow upon themselves exemptions from the very laws they expect American citizens to follow. The "two-party" system has proven to be problematic as both Democrats and Republicans take opposite sides on every issue when most Americans have a more "middle of the road" mentality. Very few Americans I talk to completely support either party's position on all topics. Most Americans are conservative on some issues and liberal on others. Our current political process does not have an alternative, and as such, voters must decide whether to support a candidate because of one issue over another. A voter who has conservative feelings about immigration but liberal feelings regarding Roe vs. Wade must decide on a candidate that does not support both. Because both parties refuse to agree on any subject or ostracize those in their party who don't toe the line on party doctrine across the board, the voters do not have the choices they deserve.

In this chapter I am going to highlight numerous issues and public opinions that dominate our political discussions and views. You will find that I am neither conservative nor liberal on all issues but have been able to find common ground on many that I feel could be resolved by Congress if they would only act in the nonpartisan fashion both claim to exhibit.

Is America divided now more than ever?

We are constantly being told that America is more divided now than at any point in American history. Listening to the media, you would think that the country is on the brink of Civil War. If we look at popular vote totals in all presidential elections since 1824 (when records of popular vote began to be recorded), the average margin of victory is approximately 7 percent. That translates to an average of 43 percent that did not support the winner or their political positions.

Some of the largest margins of victory were recorded by are as follows:

- Richard Nixon, 1972—23 percent (his margin in 1968 was only 1 percent)
- Lyndon Johnson, 1964—20 percent (his popularity fell so far he did not seek reelection in 1968)
- Franklin Roosevelt, 1936—20 percent (his popularity declined to 8 percent by 1944 due to WWII)
- Warren Harding, 1920—20 percent (America was entering the Roaring Twenties)

Some of the smallest margins (not all were victories) were recorded by are as follows:

- James Garfield, 1880—.1 percent (narrowest margin to date)
- John Kennedy, 1960—.2 percent (second narrowest margin)

- Donald Trump, 2016—.5 percent (Hillary Clinton won the popular vote)
- Grover Cleveland, 1884—.6 percent

Several including Benjamin Harrison, James Polk, Richard Nixon, and George W. Bush had margins of 1 percent. The simple fact is that the United States has always been divided on issues as is the case with every country around the globe. We decide the direction of the country at the ballot box and in the courts with the Constitution as our legal base. The negative outlook portrayed in the media about the divisiveness of the American people is significantly overstated when in fact our country was built on divided opinions and the civilized manner in the way we approach these divisions.

There are multiple issues that deeply divide the United States of America that could be included in the discussion of division, including abortion, immigration, gun control, health care, and many others. The "two-party" system failures are highlighted in these debates as neither side will concede to the majority opinion and vow to "continue the fight." This accomplishes nothing except minimizing the possibility of compromising and building a solution that all Americans can believe in and support. The division along these lines benefits the politicians and creates a perpetual platform that doesn't change or move on to addressing other issues. Roe vs. Wade is shown to be favored by 70 percent of the American population with only 24 percent believing that it should be overturned. So why after thirty-five years is this still a key plank in the Republican platform?

The same poll also shows that many Americans want some limitations. Many do not favor second and third trimester abortions. Why don't both parties get together and work out a compromise that would support the majority thinking? They would then be able to move forward to other issues. Another key point is of the 70 percent who support Roe vs. Wade, not all personally believe in abortion. Some are opposed personally but do not believe that their personal beliefs should be forced on any woman whose circumstances they may not understand. The last point I will make here is if these women were forced to have these children that they do not want, who will take care of them? What kind of life will they experience?

Immigration is another divisive topic. Immigration reform is supported by 69 percent of Americans and yet Congress does nothing. The politicians again take two opposite positions, open immigration or deport everyone here illegally. The truth is Americans want the borders sealed and the tide of undocumented aliens stopped. They do not support deporting families who have been in the United States for years illegally but have been contributing members of the American society, have not been involved in criminal activity, pay taxes, and even serve in the United States military. Those who commit crimes (excluding nonviolent misdemeanors) and those who refuse to work and expect to be supported by government programs (excluding unemployment benefits and similar benefits paid to those who contributed through work efforts) be deported. Congress should be able to reach a compromise that would protect those who have made a life in the United States, seal the borders, and protect American citizens. The simple fact is neither side is willing to compromise, a complete failure on the part of congress, equally shared by both sides. I will address gun control, term limits, and health care separately.

The idea that the United States is more divided than ever is false. The fact that our congressional representatives would rather debate the issues forever than come to a compromise for progress is the problem.

Have politicians lost their integrity?

Today only 46 percent of Americans trust their elected officials down from 66 percent when Gallup conducted the first polls between 1972 and 1976. What factors have contributed to this significant downturn in trust? I would suggest that there are multiple factors involved including scandals, disregard for the law, mudslinging, and the willingness to lie to further their own personal agendas rather than represent the will of the people. This lack of trust is not limited to one side of the political aisle as both Republicans and Democrats have seen a significant decline. Many Americans do not have trust for their own party and certainly don't for the other side.

In the past politicians on both sides were measured on the truth of their statements. This doesn't mean that if you have a different belief, say on immigration, you were considered less than truthful as differing opinions are neither right nor wrong. In society today, it is considered acceptable to lie, distort facts, and/or omit certain data points if it supports your position. *The Atlanta Journal-Constitution* publishes a "PolitiFact Truth-O-Meter" that measures the truthfulness of statements made by politicians and political commentators. I sampled statements made between 2/1/18 and 3/6/18, and the results speak for themselves:

- True—12 or 10 percent
- Mostly true—16 or 13 percent
- Half true—21 or 18 percent
- Mostly false—22 or 19 percent
- False—22 or 19 percent
- Pants on Fire—25 or 21 percent

If we say anything but *True* (completely correct without the need for additional clarification) is misleading, our politicians and commentators are deceiving the population 90 percent of the time. If we were to include *Mostly true* (substantially correct but could use some clarification), they are still deceiving us 77 percent of the time. If your friends, family, or coworkers were deceiving at this level, would you have respect for them?

To place all blame solely at the feet of the politicians would be wrong. The American population in general has become accepting of this practice and repeats these statements in support of their agendas in many cases. Those who do recognize that these statements are less than truthful, do not "call out" their representatives and make it known that false statements will not be tolerated. In fairness both parties control who will run for office, leaving the population with few options to improve the integrity of the candidates. Since a majority of citizens can see the deception (although a number only see it in the party they don't support), it is a small wonder that many question the integrity of their elected officials.

Term Limits

This is a topic that clearly demonstrates the motivation of politicians to pursue their own self-interests above the will of the people. A Gallup poll taken in January of 2013 showed that 75 percent of all Americans favored term limits. By 2016 this figure has grown to 82 percent. Despite this fact, not a single member of Congress has introduced a bill to put term limits in place. Several have begun using the issue in their campaigns to run for office, hoping to attract votes from the 82 percent. Once elected, however, that issue seems to take a back burner. In 1994 the Republican Party's "Contract with America" had term limits as a key issue. Yet despite the Republican majority at the time, the issue was ignored after the Republicans took the House and Senate. Why is that? There are multiple reasons:

- Each party supports term limits but only for the other party. Their true goal is to gain complete control of the political scene and, by default, the country.
- They have voted themselves pay raises, benefits, and special laws that make being a lifelong politician very lucrative.
- The number of loopholes and connections with lobbyists and special interest groups have made corruption, payoffs, and influence peddling easy and very financially rewarding.

There are a number of arguments that oppose term limits, and some merit can be attributed to their argument although there are steps that can be taken to eliminate the concerns.

- Elections are term limits. This would be a valid argument if the existing two-party system did not effectively limit the people who could run for office. Both parties are guilty of this limitation. To run for office as a member of either political party, the candidates *must* toe the party line. Any candidate who appears to be willing to compromise or break with the party on an issue will find themselves without funding from the party to run and in most cases will find the party heavily bankrolling a candidate who does toe the party line. Under these circumstances, candidates who may be more representative of the public's opinion have no chance of election. By having term limits in place, the senator or congressman in their last term could not be leveraged by the party leadership to vote the party line.

- Popular candidates would be required to step down. This point is true; however, this would also incent the parties to groom candidates who represented the majority opinions of their constituencies.

- You can't have an all-rookie team in Congress every few years. This is a valid point as having experienced representatives is a benefit in legislative, foreign policy, and fiscal decisions. Having reasonable term limits (twelve years for senators and representatives) provides years of experience, and since they would all not be up for reelection in the same years, there would be a constant influx of new congressional representatives mixed with more experienced legislators. Don't forget that in the State Department, and other government branches, term limits would not apply, so a very experienced and talented individual in foreign policy, for instance, could stay in service for as long as they are viable.

Term limits would provide much more benefit to the American people than career politicians currently provide. I would suggest that rather than have house representatives run every two years, their term should be three or four years. In the current two-year term, all representatives spend too much time and money on reelection rather than representing their constituents. Two six-year terms for senators and four three-year terms for representatives would be very workable.

Presidents

The most overhyped and overly criticized positions in our country's government is the President of the United States. Presidents receive accolades for economic advances, diplomatic breakthroughs, and passage of key legislature. On the other hand, they get overly criticized for economic downturns, diplomatic failures, and congressional ineffectiveness. The main problem is most Americans think that the president has far more power than given them by the Constitution. The powers of the president as defined by the constitution include the following:

- The right to sign legislation into law or veto legislation. The veto can be overridden by two-third votes of Congress.
- Commander in Chief of the Armed Forces. There are limitations on the president's authority to enter a war without a declaration from Congress. The limit of this power has been pushed and restrained over the years depending on the circumstances. For example, Franklin Roosevelt was given a lot more leeway during WWII than Bill Clinton was fifty years later.
- Appoint cabinet members and judges. Approval by Congress is required in many cases.
- Grant reprieves and/or pardons.

The president also has some "soft" powers such as:

- Negotiate treaties with foreign governments. They are not approved until ratified by two-thirds of Congress.
- Budget preparation (since 1921). The president is expected to oversee the development of the budget proposal to Congress.

Even if including the "soft powers," the office of the presidency does not hold nearly the power that the average citizen might believe. This does not mean that presidents don't have the opportunity to use other means to influence the direction of the government and our country.

The president is not permitted to introduce legislation to Congress. This does not mean that he can't persuade a member of Congress (usually in the president's party) to introduce a bill to the floor. He can also use his access to the media to try to influence the American people to support legislation. Theodore Roosevelt referred to the position as a "Bully Pulpit."

The president does not have any powers that directly impact the national economy. He does help develop the national budget, and things added or deleted from federal spending can have an impact on the economy. If there is a significant budget item to increase spending on infrastructure, the construction industry will grow, an increase in military spending might boost the aerospace, weapons production, and high-tech industries.

Taking into consideration the powers and responsibilities of the office of the presidency, *all* forty-five presidents have been successful! The problem is that many people develop their opinion of a president based on their personal feeling toward the individual rather than the performance of the job. I have listed here some relatively recent examples where the presidency was considered poor and yet each one produced key accomplishments during their presidency:

- Jimmy Carter—Many people consider his term as one of the worst by an American president although there can be no denial that he is a great humanitarian based on his works after his tenure as president. Unemployment, inflation, and high interest rates all were attributed to him although, as mentioned above, he had little impact on these issues. His failed diplomatic efforts and military action during the Iranian Embassy takeover sealed his fate. His crowning moment was the peace treaty negotiated between Israel and Egypt that still stands today nearly forty years after its signing. This treaty was a monumental accomplishment that dramatically reduced the threat of war in a region that is notoriously unstable. This tremendous achievement cannot be ignored.

- Richard Nixon—There can be no denial that his collusion in the cover-up of the Watergate break-in doomed his presidency. His repeated denials in the face of evidence caused the public (who overwhelmingly voted him into office) to turn on him and forced his resignation. It should be noted that in today's political environment, he would not have resigned and would have completed his term. Watergate did divert the attention from the things he accomplished. He got the United States out of Vietnam as he promised. He opened diplomatic relations with both the People's Republic of China and with the Soviet Union. Establishing these diplomatic relations triggered the beginning of the end of the Cold War and greatly reduced the possibility of war between superpowers.

- Barack Obama—The fact that he was the first black president elected by the American people is itself a great accomplishment that cannot be ignored. It did not translate into a great presidency as minority citizens did not see gains in economic and political clout that they had expected, and his lack of diplomatic experience hurt his foreign policy attempts. He did have two significant accomplishments. First he found and killed Osama bin Laden. Many would like to claim that he didn't have much to do with this action, but the fact remains that he had to give the final order to initiate the mission. A mission he knew was incredibly risky and could have had severe downside. The courage to give that order cannot be denied. The second was the ACA (Obamacare) elimination of the exclusion of people from coverage due to preexisting medical conditions. This outcome of the ACA is vital to ensuring ample coverage opportunity to thousands that would have otherwise been excluded from coverage.

Just as there have been presidents that have been unfairly judged, there are some who are seen in a very favorable light despite what could be described as a mediocre tenure. I have listed here some recent examples:

- John F. Kennedy—His tragic assassination led to his legacy as a great president (and rightfully so as he sacrificed his life in service to his country) despite what could be described as average performance in a short tenure. On the positive side, he introduced civil rights legislation (that many in his party did not support) that was passed after his death. He stood tall and insisted on a diplomatic solution during the Cuban Missile Crisis when many were calling for military action that could have had catastrophic consequences. On the other hand, it was the failed Bay of Pigs invasion that emboldened the Soviets and Cuban government. Kennedy also sent the first troops to Vietnam and, despite debate on his intentions, a signed order was never given to remove the troops since as commander in chief they would have been followed. In my investigation of the data available, I do believe that he considered all options from major escalation to complete withdrawal.
- Ronald Reagan—He has been hailed as a great communicator and president responsible for a ninety-two-month long economic boom, the rebuilding of the American military, and brought an end to the Cold War. He also never balanced the budget or submitted one to Congress during his terms, driving record deficits. His war on drugs was a massive failure, and he was embroiled in the Iran/Contra scandal.

My closing point here is that all presidents, regardless of popularity, have fully executed the duties of the office and have contributed something of significance to our country. It is time we all looked toward performance in office versus our perceived approval of their personality or party.

Gun Control

This is a hot button topic that has been used by politicians on both sides of the ledger to further their own agendas. Despite what the media and politicians say, America is not nearly as divided on this topic as they would have you believe. Recent polls have shown overwhelming support for the Second Amendment by the American people. The problem stems from the extreme positions taken by the opposing parties. The NRA and the far right believe that gun ownership and sales should have *no* restrictions. The far left believes that all handguns should be banned along with what they describe as "assault weapons." Neither of these positions are in line with the opinion of the American people. There are numerous issues with either extreme.

The NRA does not support any controls on the private ownership of firearms. They want you to believe that any controls are merely a step toward banning the private ownership of firearms. A majority of Americans do not share this belief and support reasonable gun controls to limit ownership to responsible individuals.

The far left would have you believe that there is no legitimate reason for any American to own firearms since we have the police and military to protect us. This ignores the fact that the Second Amendment was introduced by the founding fathers to protect us from the police and military.

Let's look at the different positions:

Making gun ownership illegal—There have been numerous instances in world history where governments banned private ownership of firearms. None of them delivered on the promise of greater safety and public security, and all led to the mass murder of citizens.

- 1911, Turkey—between 1915 and 1917, they killed ten million unarmed Armenians
- 1929, Russia—between 1929 and 1953, twenty million unarmed Russians were killed
- 1935, China—between 1948 and 1952, twenty million unarmed Chinese were killed

- 1938, Germany—between 1939 and 1946, six million unarmed Jews (and others) were killed
- 1956, Cambodia—between 1975 and 1977, one million unarmed Cambodians were killed
- 1964, Guatemala—between 1964 and 1981, one hundred thousand unarmed Mayan Indians were killed
- 1970, Uganda—between 1971 and 1979, three hundred thousand unarmed Christians were killed

There will be those who point to the gun laws in Australia passed in 1996 as an exception to the examples above. In some respect they are correct; however, Australia did not ban all weapons as legal ownership is still in place in that country.

Without guns, the ability to defend yourself from intruders, robbers, rapists, etc. is greatly diminished. The US Department of Justice reports that guns are used by citizens 1.5 million times a year to protect themselves. Almost always without a shot being fired. Some groups like to report that less than three hundred people are killed by gun owners in self-defense on an annual basis. This number is true because responsible gun owners will not discharge their firearm unless necessary. How many of the 1.5 million would have been killed or traumatized if they didn't have a firearm at their disposal?

Aside from the reasons listed above, here in the United States, other obstacles are in place. There are eighty million gun owners in the country. To compare there are only twenty-four million people in Australia. A voluntary program to turn in weapons in the United States would not work. Even if law abiding citizens turned in their weapons, the criminals most certainly would not.

Unrestricted gun ownership and purchases—there are too many reasons that this is a bad idea to list all, but I will list a few.

- Convicted felons would have easy access to weapons, and they may have already demonstrated a willingness to use deadly force in their criminal activities. This is not to say that they can't still acquire guns on the black market, but it does make it less challenging.

- Would put automatic weapons (true assault weapons) into the hands of anyone who wished to own one. No one can believe that this scenario would be a good thing. Having restrictions on these types of weapons *does* make a difference even though someone with basic armorer skills can covert a semiautomatic to full automatic with minor effort.

- Without registration of certain weapons and/or the requirement to maintain records of gun sales by dealers, law enforcement personnel would have no means of identifying the owners of firearms used in the commission of a crime. Private sales get around the restrictions, but the initial purchase information can sometimes create a trail to the owner.

Our founding fathers were very wise to enact the Second Amendment. By doing so they protected the country in a variety of ways, not all foreseen by them. They most certainly saw the danger of a large central government who could impose tyranny upon their citizens. Don't be fooled into believing that those on Capitol Hill don't take an armed citizenry into consideration. After the Kent State shooting of unarmed students protesting the war in Vietnam (by the same military that was supposed to protect them), there were those on Capitol Hill who were concerned that an armed civil war could break out. This concern led to talks and compromises that ultimately ended the Vietnam War. Without armed citizens there would have been no concern on the part of lawmakers. As another example, there were those in the Japanese military who wanted to invade the US mainland after the WWII attack on Pearl Harbor. The Japanese government decided against that action because Admiral Yamamoto warned that their troops would have been fired upon from behind every blade of grass. There have been those who dispute the fact that this is an actual quote; however, anyone with a military background would agree that an armed citizenry would have to be accounted for in any invasion plan.

How then do we support the Second Amendment and take steps to reduce gun violence? Let's explore several steps that could be taken to accomplish these goals.

- Create a "no gun" listing similar to the "no fly" listing used in the war on terror. A place where families, law enforcement, and mental health professionals can place convicted felons, those with mental health issues, and/or those who have made credible threats so they cannot buy guns. An appeal process like available in the no-fly list must be in place to prevent abuse of the process.
- Place armed guards in *all* schools, preferably police officers or former military. The most ridiculous thing we do today is proudly proclaim our schools to be "gun free zones." If you want to kill a large number of people without being fired on, where better than a school?
- Strengthen background checks and require a waiting period to purchase a firearm. It must be reasonable and should not extend beyond thirty days.
- Pass a law on private gun sales that puts some liability on the seller if the buyer uses it in the commission of a violent crime. Create a "buyback program" for citizens to sell guns to licensed gun dealers, exempting them from liability, to provide an alternative to private sales while not outlawing them.
- Strengthen penalties for licensed gun dealers who short-cut or ignore gun laws. Fines don't deter behavior, jail time does.
- Make mental health care available to those who can't afford $150/hour for treatment. Provide a vehicle for families, courts, and mental health professionals to put individuals in treatment *before* the meltdown (more on this later).

These steps would make it significantly more difficult for those who would perpetrate a mass shooting or commit a violent crime to acquire a gun. Before both sides attack these ideas, remember this, doing nothing is unacceptable and making guns illegal will do nothing (see the war on drugs). The ideas listed above would have to be carefully crafted to not interfere with our Second Amendment rights while restricting access to those not capable of making the right decisions of ownership. Unfortunately, these ideas would require non-partisan cooperation on the behalf of our lawmakers, something they have not demonstrated in the last thirty years.

Voters

If we truly look at our political process, one of our weakest links are the voters themselves. There are multiple reasons for this situation and they include the following:

- Many voters don't even register to vote. Varying reasons are given for this: I don't want to get called for jury duty, I don't have time, I don't consider myself political, my vote won't matter.
- Many voters do not investigate the issues but rely on polls, media, and rhetoric to decide on candidates and/or propositions.
- Many voters are so committed to a political party that they vote a straight ticket.
- Some voters will vote based on a single issue such as immigration, Roe vs. Wade, etc.
- Some will not vote because they don't know enough about the issues or candidates (a responsible decision).
- Voters will not call out those in their own party for misdeeds.

Voters who don't register to vote or are registered and don't vote

In the 2016 presidential election, over ninety million eligible voters did not cast a ballot. This represents 40 percent of the eligible voters. Both parties, when losing an election, will claim that low voter turnout was the reason that they lost the election. The simple fact of the matter is with over 138 million votes tallied the likelihood of a significant shift if the remaining ninety million voted is statistically unlikely. There will be those in both parties that will quote data that says they represent the majority thinking of those who didn't cast a ballot. Bear in mind that these are the same people who will quote data from polls that claim to represent the thinking of the American public when the poll surveyed one thousand participants. The winning party in any election claim to have a mandate from the people with not a mention of voter turnout. The reality is that with 138 million votes, the outcome of elections would not likely change if those who didn't vote were to cast a ballot. I would encourage every eligible voter to do so and not just in national elections. State and local government elections are in many ways more important.

Voters who don't investigate issues

I have had political discussions with individuals who don't have a complete understanding of issues but only rely on Internet/social media posts, quote facts that are partially true, and or sound alarms of serious consequences that do not appear likely to occur. When questioned about certain aspects of an issue, they often cannot respond because they only know what the sound bites have stated. Each party will publish partial truths to attempt to influence your vote (see above) by slanting the facts around any issue to favor their position. A responsible voter (almost all) will evaluate each aspect of an issue and decide based on their own personal beliefs. Many who are blinded by partisan politics will ignore the weaknesses in their position and yet point directly at the weaknesses in the opposition.

In today's voter base, many "sound bites" are quoted as fact; he's a racist, she's a socialist, he's a Muslim, etc. Claims like this without anything more than anecdotal proof only cloud the issues and deflect from real data. Voters, investigate these things on your own. The advent of the Internet doesn't just provide a platform for "fake news" or political sound bites. It also provides the ability to investigate the issues from the comfort of your home with your personal access.

Voters who vote a straight ticket by party

This is a position that I can't fault since it is based on personal choice. I would ask that those who use this method investigate issues to ensure that you still are in alignment with the party's position. Party platforms change over the years and do not always reflect the same view as in the past.

Some voters will vote based on a single issue

Although well-meaning in its intent, this is a dangerous practice, especially in national elections. Many of these voters feel very strongly about a specific issue and due to the lack of choice in a two-party system are sometimes forced to vote for a candidate they don't completely support. I admit that I understand their dilemma, but always look to what will provide the best solution to all. That being said, some issues cannot be ignored for the overall good. Human rights for all is one of those issues. I would support anyone's right to vote based on a single issue but do not believe that this is the most effective method to ensure the overall good.

Voters who don't vote because they aren't educated on the issues

I have much respect for those who readily admit that they don't understand the issues or know enough about the candidates to cast a vote. These individuals understand the importance of their vote and don't want to make a wrong choice. I would encourage all voters in this category, in any party, to take the time to investigate the candidates and issues and cast your vote based on your personal beliefs.

Voters will not call out those in their own party for misdeeds

I am continually amazed at the acceptance of misdeeds in politics by people in the same party as those committing the misdeed. During the recent Supreme Court confirmation hearing, the nominee was vilified by the opposition based on unsubstantiated claims of sexual misconduct. The same political party dismissed one of their owns' impeachment for the same issue. In the 1980s a very popular president was embroiled in an illegal arms deal. Where was the outrage from his party? It is up to the voters to hold *all* political figures accountable for their actions regardless of political affiliation. To ignore discretions just because they are in your party only emboldens them to continue.

Summary

In light of these issues, you would think that our political system is broken beyond repair. Nothing could be further from the truth. Our political process continues to guide our country to prosperity and continued freedom. The strength of our political process is the division among our citizens that is resolved at the ballot box and enforced peaceably in everyday life. The fact that people can freely speak their minds without fear of retribution for over 242 years is proof that our political process, although not perfect, works as the founding fathers envisioned.

The ability of individuals to seek and experience success based on their own drive and determination cannot be denied. This does not mean that the path will be easy. Civil rights for minorities was not an easy transition, acceptance of different lifestyles was not easy, equal status for women both in politics and business was not easy, and the list goes on. These were all hard-fought improvements, still not completely done, in our society. Every election we see new strides being made in minority representation, women in political office, and changes in the political landscape. I would encourage everyone to participate in the political process and insist that our representatives enforce the will of the people.

Health Care

No one can question the importance of health care as it impacts all in society regardless of political affiliation, race, religion, national origin, or economic status. Health care is rarely thought about or discussed until it's needed. Younger people are never overly concerned about health care as most rarely even see a doctor. When I was in my twenties, I would go three years at a time without seeing a doctor. The older I got, the more I became interested in health care options. Two things drove the interest. First was my kids were born and regular trips to the pediatrician were required for checkups, immunizations, and the treatment of minor injuries. The second was as I reached certain age milestones, the introduction of specific tests and an annual physical became necessary. In this chapter I will address the cost, the availability, and the effectiveness of our health care system. I will also explore topics like immunizations, medical malpractice, and the role of insurance companies in the process.

First let's discuss the progress made in the medical field over the last one hundred years. Although people today often claim our health today is not good because of pollutants, GMOs, food additives, and poor diet; the fact remains that people today live far longer and live more active lives than their ancestors did one hundred years ago. I have outlined a comparison of the leading causes of death from the early 1900s to 2016:

	Year 1900	Year 2016
Pneumonia	154,218	49,226
	200 per 100,00	15 per 100,000
Tuberculosis	147,828	528
	194 per 100,000	.2 per 100,000

	Year 1900	Year 2016
Measles	10,668	0
	14 per 100,000	
Mumps	91,440	0
	120 per 100,000	
Diphtheria	30,480	0
	40 per 100,000	
Typhoid Fever	24,384	0
	32 per 100,000	
Dysentery	9,144	0
	12 per 100,000	

The reduction in deaths per year of 418,408 is one of the main reasons the average life expectancy increased from forty-seven years in 1900 to over seventy-two years in 2016 as many of these diseases killed children and young adults. In addition to these diseases, other afflictions such as polio and smallpox have been eradicated. Smallpox alone killed over three hundred million worldwide in the twentieth century. The advances made in cancer research have significantly improved the survival rate, and new techniques in heart health have extended the lives of many. There can be no doubt that the improvements in health care technology and science have made a significant difference in the lives of all.

Despite the desire to provide adequate health care to everyone, it is not a right. It is a service provided by those seeking compensation. This means that not all can always afford the care they need and is one of the major points of discussion in society today. Universal health care is practiced in many countries with mixed results. The same can be said for free market health care. In either case some do not get the care they need in a timely fashion.

Universal vs. Market-Based Programs

Universal health care is practiced in many industrialized countries today. Despite the utopic vision of health care available to all, it does not come without drawbacks.

- Significant increase in taxes to cover the expense. Bernie Sanders' proposal during the 2016 presidential campaign suggested an increase in taxes between 2.2 percent for individual families with an income below $250,000 and a 6.7 percent increase to businesses. Claims that universal health care would benefit small business have not been proven, and some economists claim the increased taxes would cause layoffs and profit pressure for many small businesses.
- Wait time for services would be extended. In the industrialized nations with universal health care, the average wait time to see a specialist is 21.2 weeks. Patients who would have been fine with access to care immediately sometimes die while waiting. Laura Hillier of Ontario, Canada, needed a bone marrow transplant, had a donor, and was forced to wait for available hospital time. She died after waiting for months. Brain Booy of the UK was diagnosed in July 1997 with angina and needed a triple bypass. He died in January 1999 while still on the waiting list for the surgery. Over fifty-two thousand Canadians travel out of country, on an annual basis, to pay for out-of-pocket health care (most to the USA). I personally worked with several Canadians who told me that the only reason they were in the USA was for health care availability.
- Universal health care reduces competition which in turn slows innovation. The standardization of fees and bureaucracy associated with new services slows medical breakthroughs and their introduction to the public.

Market-based health care as practiced in the United Sates is not without drawbacks.

- Health care is not available to all, especially preventive care which can prevent more serious health care events. Roughly 11 percent of Americans are without health insurance and are at greater risk for health issues. Although people in a medical crisis are not turned away from emergency rooms, they often do not get adequate aftercare that can have disastrous results. I must point out that the cost of these uninsured patients represents only 3 percent of our total health care expenditures. A significant amount for sure but not the crisis insinuated in the media.
- Medical insurance companies want to exclude those with preexisting conditions such as cancer, heart disease, diabetes, etc. This is simply because the insurance companies do not care about your health, only making a profit. Fortunately the ACA (Affordable Care Act) eliminated this abomination. If insurance companies want to sell health insurance, they must be required to insure all at a reasonable cost.
- Medical insurance companies want to dictate your treatment. They hire doctors to advise them as to whether a patient needs a particular procedure. These doctors are hardly unbiased since their income is derived from the insurance companies. The opinion of the attending physician should be paramount.
- Emergency rooms are inundated with uninsured patients with noncritical injuries or illness which stresses the resources of hospitals as they attempt to focus on true emergencies.
- There is a lack of concentration on controlling the cost of medical services as the insurance companies will simply raise their premiums to offset rising expenses. This is an annual event as insurance premiums have risen every year.

Both scenarios place someone between the doctors and the patients. In universal care it is the government, and in market-based care it is the insurance companies. What is lost in these scenarios is the ability of the doctors to make decisions directly with patients without third party involvement. A doctor may want to run a specific test that the third party deems "not necessary." Without third party involvement, the doctor, knowing the patient's financial situation, may elect to charge significantly less for his services to someone who can't afford the standard rate (a common event prior to the introduction of medical insurance). Third party scenarios create a situation where no one is held accountable. The next time your insurance provider declines a test or procedure, contact them and see if you can reach anyone who can waive that decision (I won't hold my breath).

How then do we resolve this conflict? Let's take the best of both worlds and develop a system that delivers the best of both. The ACA, despite its detractors, has been able to provide coverage to over sixteen million people that did not have coverage prior to the implementation of ACA. I believe that this benefit can't be ignored. I will admit that the ACA itself could use some modification to improve coverage and expand acceptance (too many health care providers still don't accept it), but it must not be repealed leaving sixteen million without coverage. Most importantly the mandate to eliminate pre-existing conditions must not be overturned. Although I see that our legislators have no problem launching investigations into the opposing party representatives or their dealings, none apparently have the backbone to investigate the insurance companies. Don't believe for a moment that these companies embraced ACA. They would love to see it repealed as it mandates a lower profit margin program, and their goal is profit (rightfully so but not at the expense of those who need the assistance). Notice that I said lower margin, not a loss. I feel very confident that a system can be developed that maximizes coverage and allows for free market benefit.

Last I will address the question, "Should everyone be covered?" There are those individuals who will not pay for coverage even if it is affordable. They elect to use their money elsewhere. Most of these individuals are young and see the expense as unnecessary and feel that they never need to see a doctor anyway. Those who can afford coverage but refuse it are making a personal decision and should be required to live with this decision. Is this cruel? What if someone starved to death because they refused to buy food even though they could afford it? Should we be required to feed them? What about those who can't afford it? I find it difficult to believe that the brightest minds in Congress, executives at the insurance companies, and medical professionals cannot develop a program to address those who literally cannot afford medical coverage or services. The key here would be to stop the "take it or leave it" attitude demonstrated by both sides and compromise where needed to provide the best possible solution. The issue they must solve is how do you prevent those who can afford coverage/services from taking advantage of the program. I would not want to see someone with a $1,000 smart phone, $150 sneakers, and driving a new car in line at a program for indigent people in need of the services.

Mental Health

The greatest deficiency in medical care today is the lack of adequate coverage for mental health issues. Mental health issues have carried a stigma of personal weakness for far too long. It has been clearly proven that people can't just "get over it" when facing mental health issues. Some of these issues are nonlife threatening and some clearly have very serious consequences when left untreated. In 2017 alone 47,173 individuals committed suicide in the United States. It is the tenth leading cause of death in the United States. Many of these could have been prevented with adequate treatment options. Mass shootings have been a prominent topic for the news media and political discussion. Since 1982 there have been 106 mass shootings (defined as any shooting with three or more deaths) that have killed 865 and injured 1,337. In most of these cases, particularly the nine incidents that account for 28 percent of the deaths and 58 percent of the injured, the perpetrators clearly had mental health issues.

Nikolas Cruz, the Parkland Florida shooter, had two mental health professionals recommend involuntary admission to a mental health facility. The mental institution concluded he was a low risk to harm himself or others despite forty 911 calls bringing law enforcement to his residence. It should be noted that he purchased his firearms legally, and there was no record of his mental issues found during his background checks. James Holmes, the Aurora Colorado shooter, began having mental health issues in middle school and attempted suicide at age eleven. He had met with three mental health professionals while at the University of Colorado, and two considered him to be a threat. Dr. Lynne Fenton told campus police that he made homicidal statements one month before the shooting. So why were these individuals not admitted to a mental institution prior to the commission of their crimes?

The events that explain these situations began in the 1800s with the introduction of "insane" asylums. It was believed in those times that the best treatment for mental illness was to segregate them from society for their protection and the protection of society in general. This was a noble idea; however, over the course of the 1800s and into the 1900s, these institutions became known more for their cruelty and abuse rather than the compassionate treatment of the mentally ill. In addition the ability of these institutions to collude with families and courts to institutionalize individuals without due cause and little if any recourse for those caught in this trap became a national scandal. Many of the treatments for mental health issues known today were not known at the time, so recovery was not guaranteed and many individuals institutionalized were, in essence, given a life sentence.

How do we protect both the rights of the individual and public safety? I would suggest that a program that outlines different avenues depending on the perceived seriousness of the situation. In the case of potential violence, law enforcement, parents and/or family members, and medical professionals must have the ability to involuntarily detain those who show signs, make threats, or appear to be preparing to commit violent acts. Although this option is available today, it is rarely used, and the guidelines for what constitutes a threat to others is too loosely defined. This puts an enormous burden on those asked to evaluate the level of threat.

Following the Parkland shooting, the names of the officers, arrest records, 911 calls were all made public. Why weren't the names of those who determined he wasn't a threat, despite overwhelming evidence, released? Personally I am glad they didn't release these names as their safety could have been compromised had they been publicly identified. I would also imagine that these individuals will have to live with their decision, a far worse fate. Here are some steps I believe would improve our ability to prevent these situations:

- Enact legislation that allows medical professionals, law enforcement, and family members to have a potentially violent individual involuntarily committed to a psychiatric facility. There must be some evidence of this threat, such as erratic/delusional behavior with threats of violence, weapons availability, previous violent acts, etc.
- Mandate an initial review by trained physicians within seventy-two hours to determine if the individual poses a threat. These guidelines must be stringent and not allow for the release of those who "might not" be a threat. No one who interviewed the Parkland shooter believed that he did not have mental health issues.
- The facilities to treat these individuals must be closely monitored to ensure the individuals are getting the *proper* care, not just being medicated into oblivion.
- Appeals procedures for those committed must be available to ensure the commitment is valid.
- Regularly scheduled reviews of those involuntarily committed to review treatment progress, quality of care, and the validity of continued incarceration must be scheduled in a timely manner (I would suggest every three months) and include family members as well as the medical staff.

I am not saying that all mass shootings since 1982 would have been prevented by these steps, but a significant number might have been prevented. For this process to succeed, it *must* be properly funded. Too many health care initiatives fail because of perceived expense. Facilities, medical personnel, and proper oversight are required to launch a process of this type.

What about the nonviolent individuals struggling with mental health issues? Too many of them end up incarcerated or homeless without treatment options. Many are veterans struggling with the aftermath of their deployments to war zones (shame on the Veterans Administration). Others may be individuals with a family history of afflictions such as depression, bipolar disorder, schizophrenia, and others too numerous to list here. Why do we ignore the needs of these people? How many of those suffering would get the treatment they need if it was readily available? I will say that the insurance companies have addressed the availability of mental health care by covering counseling to a certain level. I do think that this level is inadequate for those with more serious, deeply rooted afflictions. Outpatient options for individuals without medical coverage must be addressed in any national health care initiative.

I wouldn't want anyone to read this and think that I am attacking the mental health professionals who work diligently to help many of the individuals outlined above. I believe that they do not have the necessary resources to handle the mental health issues present in society today. How many suicides could be prevented? Improvement of just 10 percent would result in nearly five thousand lives saved annually.

Medical Malpractice

According to statistics published by Johns Hopkins University, 250,000 deaths occur due to medical errors in the United States on an annual basis. This sounds like an astronomical number until you consider the number of medical decisions made in the country on an annual basis. Even a conservative estimate of two hundred million medical decisions (two-third of the population making one visit a year with one decision) would mean that the right decision is made

99.9 percent of the time. Still if you are one of those impacted, you would want to know what could be done to prevent these unfortunate deaths. The AMA and medical care administrations place a significant focus on eliminating as many of these as possible, yet they still occur. Is it reasonable to think that all these deaths can be prevented? Even as someone untrained in the field, I can determine that is not possible. This is not to say that this statistic can't be improved. A number of these deaths are caused by physicians who are not competent in their skill set and make bad decisions as a result. Many, however, are not the result of negligence and are simply the result of a very complex field that changes daily and, in some instances, taking a risk as the only way to potentially save a patient.

Doctors are put into a very delicate situation as medicine is not always an exact science. There are risky procedures, and patients and families are told of risks involved but still sometimes sue the doctor because a patient died. The only problem I have here is the medical profession resembles law enforcement, and the "blue wall" and doctors who don't have the necessary skills or are negligent practice far too long before being reported by other doctors. Doctors who sexually abuse patients or commit Medicare fraud have their license revoked far faster than those who perform poorly. In addition states regulate the medical profession, and if you have your license revoked in one state, you can go to another and get licensed in the new state. What can the average patient do to ensure that the doctor is not negligent or have had their license revoked in another state?

- There are databases online that identify doctors that have had their license revoked.
- Get referrals from friends, coworkers, and family to doctors they have used. Doctors with long-term patients have been doing something right.
- Use a doctor experienced in treating your specific problem. There's a reason that professional athletes all seem to go to the same doctor for specific treatments.

- Avoid doctors who only spend a couple of minutes with you or don't allow you to fully describe the problem. They are overbooked and more likely to make a misdiagnosis.
- Don't be afraid to get a second opinion. Good doctors encourage it, bad doctors are insulted.

The overwhelming majority of those in the medical field work to a very high standard of ethics and performance. It does not mean that they are infallible, and there are times when a patient will die despite best efforts of the medical staff. My father died of a massive heart attack at age fifty-three one week after having a complete physical and given a clean bill of health. His doctor was one of his best friends and was out with him when it happened. Should he have seen this coming? Should I have sued him for malpractice? I can tell you from my conversation with him that he was nearly as distraught as I. Nothing during that physical indicated a problem. It was just my father's time.

Immunizations

I have read with great interest over the last forty years as people have begun to question the need for immunizations. When you consider some of the statistics presented earlier in this chapter of diseases that no longer cause deaths, I find this question puzzling at best.

A recent outbreak of measles that began in Washington State and Oregon quickly spread to other states and infected over seventy in less than a month. Most of these were children, but some were over eighteen years of age. All those who contracted the disease were unvaccinated. These outbreaks and others (Brooklyn, New York) all began in pockets of low vaccination rates. Washington and Oregon are states with very liberal rules for parents to opt out of vaccinations. In the Brooklyn outbreak, it began in the Orthodox Jewish community due to religious beliefs.

I realize that this is a sensitive subject, but those who refuse vaccinations are not just exposing their children to risk. Parents in these areas are afraid to bring infants to day care or take them out to public areas for fear of contracting measles or other diseases controlled by vaccinations as their children are, at this point, too young to have received the vaccinations. It is just a matter of time before a lawsuit is filed against an anti-vaxxer for infecting another. I am more understanding of those who have religious concerns, but they represent a very small number of the total population. The exercise of religious freedom certainly is valid but should not screen you from legal responsibility for spreading the disease.

I have read where parents make the decision based on the number of cases in the United States and attempt to project whether the risk for harm is greater from the vaccine or the possibility of contracting the disease. Sounds good, doesn't it? What about these factors below?

- What happens if your adult child travels to another country and contracts the disease?
- With international travel so commonplace today, what if someone brings the disease to your community?
- How would you feel if your child is the one who contracts the disease and dies?

    Tragically a couple in the UK had to deal with this when their unvaccinated child contracted the measles and died.

Although I vaccinated my children, I am reluctant to mandate immunizations for all. That said I also believe that governments have the right to mandate such provisions as a requisite to use public facilities. I believe each individual has the right to make this decision based on their religious beliefs and other factors, but I would expect them to use actual proven data, not rhetoric from some celebrity or a study proven to be false. The reality is very few have any adverse reaction to immunizations. The most common is allergic reaction, and they rarely have any significant result.

I understand that parents want to shield their children from all possible risk. While this sounds admirable, it is an impossible goal.

Life creates risk. Every time your child is in a car, he/she is at greater risk than from vaccines. Playing sports, swimming, teaching them to drive, all involve greater risk than vaccines. Life is full of risk, but if you attempt to avoid all risk, you cannot live life to the fullest.

In closing this chapter on health care, I would like for people to consider these facts:

- People live longer and healthier lives as a result of progress in the field of medicine.
- Doctors are not gods; they are extremely dedicated individuals who save lives on a daily basis. Unfortunately, they can't save everyone they treat.
- We are *all* going to die at some point. It can't be prevented, but there are things we can do to improve our quality of life and otherwise extend it to a full term.

I would ask our officials in government, business, and health care to get together and *compromise* to develop a system that provides the best health care possible. We will never cover all as some will resist, but we can certainly improve on the current situation.

Science

One of the most debated subjects in the history of mankind, and rightfully so, is science. The basic premise of science is to explore new theories and gain understanding of the world around us and even into the cosmos as we expand space exploration. Scientists, since the beginning of recorded history, have been both exalted and scorned as they challenged thinking and proposed ideas that the general population, and other scientists, sometimes dismissed as they disputed current thinking. In these scenarios, both sides have had wins and losses. The simple fact that some theories were proven to be true and others were proven to be incorrect is the genesis for scientific advancement. Let's look back at some theories that were generally accepted at the time but were ultimately proven to be incorrect.

- The Earth is flat.
- The sun revolves around the earth.
- Heavier than air-flying machines are impossible.
- The power of the atom can never be harnessed.

All these theories were proven to be incorrect through scientific study although the scientists who conducted these studies were often ridiculed at the time. Scientific advancements are not possible without opposing opinions. To challenge current thinking is the foundation of science.

Over the course of history scientists developed what is called the "scientific method" to prove or disprove theories. In many cases this method will prove the theory to be correct and allow the theory to become scientific law. In some cases the scientific method is unable to prove the theory true or false. In those cases it remains a theory until it can be proven.

In today's society scientists working in various fields of study are at an all-time high. They include the field of medicine, engineering, the environment, electronics, space exploration, agriculture, and many others. This has driven the advancement of technology and scientific breakthroughs at a breakneck pace. Unfortunately, it has also caused an overload of unproven theories to become accepted by the general population. Even though some of these theories are debunked, they still linger in the minds of some individuals. Other theories have not been proven or disproven and generate much debate.

Climate Change

This topic is the most debated scientific subject today. Both sides have provided countless studies that look at the current situation and provide data to support their position. Both sides claim that they have "proven" their position, but the reality remains that neither side reached the burden of proof required by the scientific method. The resulting debates and predictions of dire consequences in the near future ratchet up the dialogue to denial by both sides of valid points that would move this science forward. The use of computer models by both also fans the flames although everyone should agree that a computer model that can accurately predict weather events has not been created.

I want to be sure to point out that I believe the phenomena of climate change should continue to be studied to gather additional data on actual results. The main problem that many have on this subject is the limited sample size of the data gathered. The Earth has been around for millions of years, and we have roughly one hundred years of data to predict the future. This translates to .000001 percent sample of the Earth's data over the last one hundred million years. To put this in perspective, to predict the next president of the United States, we would only have to poll 350 voters. How confident would you be with the results of this poll? Would you suggest the election would be unnecessary based on this result? No one would agree to this scenario.

I have listed below some facts regarding the climate change:

- The Earth is actually warming since 1900. We have solid data to support the conclusion that the Earth is warming by .15 degrees Fahrenheit per decade. That equals 1.5 degrees per one hundred years. In five hundred years, we would see an increase of 7.5 degrees.
- In 1970, many scientists were predicting a new ice age coming due to pollution.
- The level of the oceans has risen by .1 inch per year since 1900. That equals ten inches per one hundred years. In five hundred years, we would see an increase of fifty inches.
- Glaciers are shrinking worldwide, but they have been shrinking for several hundred years before the introduction of CO_2 caused by humans. They have been shrinking since the end of the last ice age 11,500 years ago.
- Claims that 40 percent of existing species would become extinct because of an average temperature change of four degrees have not been proven; however, it should be noted that 99.9 percent of all species in the history of our planet are now extinct. Scientists estimate that there are between ten and fourteen million species on the planet today. The claim that this small change in temperature would cause a massive extinction flies in the face of evolutionary science. For example, polar bears are frequently used as an example of a species at risk. Let's say that they are at risk. There are reports of polar bears crossbreeding with brown bears now that their respective ranges overlap. Is this the result of evolution with the end result being a bear more adaptable to the new environment?
- The National Oceanic and Atmospheric Administration documented that recent history has shown a decrease in major weather events (hurricanes). During the years 2016–

2018, there were six hurricanes that reached landfall and caused over a billion dollars in damages. During the years 2003–2005, there were nine hurricanes to reach landfall and cause over a billion dollars in damages. Those who use the dollar value of damages to compare decades must be cautious because of differing circumstances. Significantly more people and businesses are located in coastal areas that can be impacted by hurricanes today than was the case thirty years ago. The costs must also be adjusted for inflation (and many are) to show comparisons.

- CO_2 levels were 5–7 times higher during the last ice age than they are today. Based on current data, all species should have become extinct before they had a chance to evolve. The high levels of CO_2 enhanced the warming and accelerated the end of the ice age.

- CO_2 is *not* pollution. It is vital to life on earth. Some have predicted that climate change and rising CO_2 levels would have a negative impact on crop production and severely reduce food supplies. The fact is that global crop production is at an all-time high. Additional CO_2 enhances plant growth.

- Solar activity contributes to climate change but is not the only cause. Scientists believe that the sun is moving to a minimal activity phase which they predict will reduce the average temperature by .5 degrees. They also warn that it would move toward a maximum activity level once it reaches the minimum and temperatures would again rise.

I could go on for a significant time listing these points on both sides of the argument, but they only enhance my position that neither side has proven their position. Based on data there can be no question that the environment is changing. The question becomes how much is it changing? How much of this change is man-made? Are these changes part of the normal evolution of the planet? What will the impact of these changes have on life on earth?

Until these questions can be answered and *proven*, we should continue to fund research, collect data, and implement changes proven to have an impact on climate change. Considering the fact that current trends and data do not support predictions of impending doom, both sides of the argument should work together to study the issue. The proposals that would cripple industry, economies, and cause a deterioration of quality of life for the people of Earth should not be supported considering that the data tells us we would not see significant impact for several hundred years. It is time for both sides to take a step back and truly evaluate how to proceed. Politicians and alarmists love to predict doom to scare people to support their position. Don't fall for that tactic. The other issue is related to the world itself. The United States could implement every protocol suggested to stop climate change, and it would be worthless unless the other industrialized nations of the world implemented them as well. Recent history has shown that they will not damage their own economies and standard of living to support a theory not yet proven by the scientific method.

Biased Science

The proliferation of scientific study and those involved in science research has created a wealth of scientific discovery and activity. One of the unfortunate by-products of this is the use of what I refer to as "biased science." This is defined as using scientific data to support a given position or agenda and omitting any data that might put your position in an unfavorable light. This is not a new phenomenon but has seemed to explode over the past few decades as funding, social media, and political access have increased dramatically in the digital age. The problem with biased science is the opportunity for people to think certain facts quoted are true when in reality they may only be half true or completely false.

One more recent "fact" quoted that illustrates this situation was, "More greenhouse gases were emitted into the atmosphere during the Mt. St. Helens eruption than emitted by all the cars in the history of mankind." The reality is cars worldwide emit the same amount of greenhouse gases in just a few days. I remember that in the early 1970s, a study on the effects of hashish use was proven to cause cancer. The problem with this study was in order to generate the cancerous tumor in lab rats, the rats were forced to ingest a quantity that would have been the equivalent of a person smoking a chunk of hashish the size of a kitchen table every day for a year. Their conclusion was hardly relevant.

The problem with biased science is that opinions can be incorrectly swayed by the publication of biased and/or flawed data. One of the most damaging in my opinion was the study done in 1998 by Andrew Wakefield and twelve colleagues in the UK that linked MMR vaccinations to autism. This study was quickly discredited, and ten of the twelve colleagues issued a retraction that stated no causal effect of the vaccinations on autism was found. In addition the British Medical Journal exposed the study as fraud for financial gain. The study used a sample size not satisfactory to quantify results, and the study was funded by lawyers representing parents in a lawsuit with the drug companies. Despite these developments, some anti-vaxxers still quote this study to justify their position.

Why would scientists be a part of this methodology? It could be that they support the agenda they are trying to prove and slant/omit data to win at any cost. It could be as simple as money. They are paid by a third party to conduct a study that delivers a specific result. Is this a bad practice? Not really as all research and scientific study has value, not to mention how many significant discoveries have been "accidentally" found. It does highlight the fact that you should look at all scientific claims with a skeptical eye. Too many people believe that they are not knowledgeable enough to question scientists. Not true in any sense. First most people have a built in "bull poop" detector. If it sounds like it doesn't make sense to you, investigate! Look at how the study was conducted. Was it done in an unbiased manner? Did they review both sides of the issue thoroughly? Does the study mirror real life?

Here are some guidelines to evaluate the studies:

- If possible, get the full results of the study to review.
- Does it pass the "sniff test"? Does the conclusion of the study seem plausible?
- Were assumptions made without supporting data?
- Find opposing viewpoints and compare to the study.
- Who funded the study? Do they have reason to bias the results?

    They might have a very official sounding name but could be a single individual or small biased group. Even if a large group such as the approximately thirty thousand climate scientists who support the climate change conclusions, you have to ask yourself, how many of those thirty thousand are being paid based on the assumption that the theory is correct? Do you think this could bias their opinion? As I mentioned earlier, their data certainly supports further research.

The one thing I would like to get across here is the fact that everyone has the capability of deciding for themselves if they believe a scientific claim. Be especially skeptical of the headlines that predict near term dire consequences. If you do a little research (it only took me fifteen minutes to discover that the Mt. St. Helens "fact" was incorrect) and look at the data with an open mind, you will always appear to be very well versed on the subject at hand no matter which side of the issue you support.

Education

Education is not typically debated on a national scale with the exception of the occasional headline stating that American students are way behind other nations in educational performance. Education is viewed as a more localized topic as local property taxes fund local school districts with allocated federal funds distributed locally. This process has both advantages and disadvantages that I will discuss in this chapter. Let's begin by stating the goal of education. It would seem that the goal of education would be multifold.

- Prepare the students for life in today's society.
- Provide options to allow students to determine their career path and study accordingly.
- Teach fundamental and advanced skills in math, social studies, science, literature, language, etc.
- Develop reasoning skills to enable students to evaluate data and solve complex problems through deductive reasoning.
- Develop interpersonal skills by working with other students on projects and assignments in teams and debating results in a respectful, factual manner.

These goals seem very reasonable, but are they being reached? Who has the responsibility to ensure that these goals are being met? Are all students capable of learning any discipline? What should students be taught? These questions and others will be addressed in this chapter.

What should be taught?

In today's society many believe that all students should be taught the same subjects in the same way to ensure that all students have an equal opportunity to succeed. Does this really make sense? I believe that to a certain point in the educational cycle this does make some sense. Certainly students in grades K to sixth while learning basic math, language, science, and history would seem to thrive in this environment. However, by the completion of the sixth grade, it has become apparent that some students excel more than others in certain academic arenas. Beginning in middle school, there should be some choices in education moving forward. Aside from those who will be going to college (only one in three will get a four-year degree), what educational training for the remaining students is available to prepare them for a career?

First let's explode the myth that if you don't graduate from college, you'll earn significantly less than your college-educated peers. I have seen studies that show "average" wages of those who attained a four-year degree being a certain percentage higher that those who did not get a degree. The key word is average.

Here are a few incredibly rich individuals who did not graduate from college:

- Bill Gates/Paul Allen—founded Microsoft
- Russell Simmons—music/Hip-Hop
- Walt Disney—entertainment/theme parks
- Mark Zuckerberg—founded Facebook
- Oprah Winfrey—entertainment/entrepreneur
- Coco Channel—fashion
- Brad Pitt—movies

There are thousands of examples of others who did not go to college but found success in construction, vehicle maintenance, electrical contracting, food service, plumbing, art/sculpting, law enforcement, farming, broadcasting, and too many others to list here. Does this minimize the importance of a college education? Not in the slightest! Many careers are predicated on education such as doctors, lawyers, engineers, and many others who must complete significant educational requirements before being licensed in their field. The completion of a degree in some disciplines would not even guarantee a job. That said additional training and education in *any* field is certainly beneficial. What it does imply is that we need to stop telling our children that they have to get a traditional college degree to be successful. There are a number of avenues to be successful in the world today. The one key common denominator is hard work. Let's look at some alternatives to our current system.

Reintroduce training in crafts like auto shop, woodworking, sewing, cooking, etc. These high school training programs should feed directly into technical schools who should be accredited just like any university. Completion of that training would prepare these individuals to embark on a career that will allow them to support themselves and their families and embrace the American dream.

Strengthen and/or return to teaching the principles of our government. Too many young people I speak to today don't understand the intricacies of our government. It is important to recognize the difference between a republic, a democracy, a monarchy, a dictatorship, and a socialist government. I find it interesting that many people believe that the United States is a democracy (we are a republic with democratically elected representatives).

Introduce life-training programs to prepare students to handle adult situations. Some of these classes could include the following:

- Budgeting and personal finances—teach students how to set up household budgets and invest in savings. How to buy a car or home, file taxes, and manage credit.
- How to start a business—building customer base, securing financing, understanding your market, and creating business plans.
- Negotiation—many things in life must be negotiated, but it is not a discipline taught to students. They are left to learn on their own, usually by losing a negotiation with less than favorable consequences.

The addition or enhancement of these training examples would certainly better prepare high school graduates for entry into society.

Common Core

Common Core is one of the most discussed issues in precollege education today. It is also one of the most misunderstood. The general belief is that Common Core tells school administrators what to teach and how to teach. This is simply not the case. The problem with this process is how it is administered. Having minimum competency levels for students as they progress through elementary to high school is the right idea. The problem comes with the question, "How do you measure it?" The obvious answer for most people is "test results." If we link financial issues, such as teacher pay, school funding, and school ranking to the test results exclusively, the goal of education changes from learning the content to passing the tests. The focus of the students becomes memorization of facts on the test rather than developing an in-depth understanding of the topic. This has a negative impact on retention of the concepts and understanding of the topic.

My take on Common Core is it is a valuable tool to establish a minimum level of competency for students at each level. I believe that it should be used as a guideline and should not have the financial implications associated with it today. Allowing the teachers to ensure the concepts are understood by the students rather than relying on test scores benefits the students to a greater degree. I can remember multiple occasions where I had teachers divert from the basic lesson plan to discuss a topic in great detail that significantly increased my understanding of the topic. Mr. Kovinick, one of my favorite teachers, did this many times in my high school civics class. To this day I can remember these discussions and how he taught all of his students to intelligently debate key topics with respect for the other person.

No Child Left Behind (not the legislation)

How can a statement that sounds so good be so bad? No one would argue that no child should be left behind, but what does "left behind" mean? Does it mean that the student should be promoted with his/her class even if they did not complete the work or understand the curriculum? I would argue that if they didn't complete the work or understand the curriculum and are being passed to the next level, they *are* being left behind. How will they be expected to complete the next level of learning if they don't have a good foundation from the last level? Making students repeat a grade if necessary does more good than harm. It ensures that they will have an opportunity to learn the curriculum they will need at the next level, it provides them with motivation to ensure that they will earn promotion to the next level, and it teaches them to face setbacks in life.

The fact that students know they will be promoted to the next level even if they fail discourages students from putting in the work they need to succeed. We are teaching them that they will succeed even if they don't put in the effort. This mentality in the workforce means difficulty in holding jobs and blaming others for their failures.

The reason educators have provided for this practice include the following:

- It would place a stigma on the student who was forced to repeat the grade. When did the goal of education become protecting feelings rather than learning?
- The students' confidence could be damaged by being held back. Is the students' confidence going to soar in the next year when they fall further behind?
- The parents would be upset and complain. Are they upset because they believe this reflects poorly on them? Are they concerned that their child has not gained the necessary knowledge to advance?
- Schools can't afford to educate students for the additional terms. This should not be a consideration.

Do any of these reasons really benefit the students? In my opinion failure to ensure students learn the curriculum creates lifelong hardships for them and far outweighs any embarrassment the student or their parents may experience. We should work to reduce the stigma by recognizing that all students do not learn at the same pace. Some can quickly absorb concepts while others may require more time. The important fact is that they *learn* what they need to learn, and it is not based on how fast they learned.

In order to minimize this situation, schools must pay special attention to those who might struggle to keep up (many schools have these programs in place) and provide tutoring, study halls, parental involvement, and lots of encouragement to these students. The goal is to minimize the need to hold a student back.

Teachers

There tends to be a willingness to blame teachers for the failures of our school systems to properly educate students. Nothing could be further from the truth. I know many teachers (including my sister, granddaughter, and niece), and teachers are singularly one of the most dedicated professions in the country today. No one enters the field of education with the expectation of getting rich as educator pay is disgustingly low, considering the importance of their task. Many, due to funding issues, spend their own limited money to buy necessary supplies for their classrooms. They work incredibly long hours (although some do have an extended summer vacation), deal with constantly changing rules and regulations, with unruly and sometimes violent students, unreasonable parents, and less than adequate facilities. This does not mean all teachers are inspirational mentors that get the most out of their students' potential. Some are more talented than others as in every profession. When I was in school, I had a number of teachers that stood out as inspirational and many that just taught the curriculum effectively. I can only think of a couple that I felt didn't really care, and amazingly enough I learned enough in their classes to still understand and pass the class.

The ability of the teachers to educate is also dependent on the resources at their disposal. The current process for funding schools plays a major role in this discrepancy (more on that later in this chapter). Poorer schools can't afford expensive computer labs, newer textbooks, competitive salaries, and extra activities such as field trips. This creates an uneven playing field when comparing results from more affluent schools. Leveling this playing field is critical to creating an equal opportunity for learning at all schools.

Teachers are also expected to teach things traditionally taught by parents at home. Manners, respect for others, sex education, morals, and social interaction skills. Teachers do not have the time to individually teach these things to students. On top of that fact, if they were required to teach these skills, do their opinions on these topics mirror those of the parents? Certainly not in all cases. These values must be taught at home.

To believe that the teachers are responsible for the many issues in our education system is ill founded. They provide the opportunity for students to learn. It is up to the students to take advantage of the opportunity.

Parents

Parents, like it or not, play the most important role in educating our children. Parental involvement in the education of their child can overcome every obstacle listed in this chapter. There are too many examples of students excelling at school in impoverished districts because the parent(s) were involved and insisted that their child succeed. There are also too many instances of students from affluent backgrounds failing miserably because of indifference on the part of parent(s).

Parents must be more involved to ensure the success of the child's education. Some of the reasons I have heard for lack of involvement include the following:

- I don't have time with work and all of my other priorities. This is problematic for a couple of reasons. First it doesn't take that much time to stay in contact with your child's educators. Attend an open house and meet your child's teachers. In today's world of texting, e-mailing, and checking school-sponsored parent portals, it is easy to monitor progress. The fact that I could go onto a parent portal daily and check grades, status of assignments, etc. was definitely a motivator for one of my children. Partner with the teachers to ensure success.

- I can't help because I don't understand the subject. Boy, have we all experienced that dilemma especially in the higher grades! Just because you don't understand doesn't mean you can't help. Many schools have tutoring programs you can use to get extra instruction for your child. Private companies and tutors are also available although at some expense (not as much as you might expect). Without tutoring one of my children would not have graduated high school on time.

- I can't make them study or apply themselves, so what's the use? If you, as the parent, can't make them participate in their education, why believe a teacher in a classroom setting is going to accomplish this task? It is important to note that there are parents who *are* involved but due to other factors (ADHD, emotional issues, etc.) have difficulty keeping their child focused on their education.

Interestingly enough parents can also be too involved. The "helicopter parents" who insist that their child pursue education in areas of little interest or push them to succeed beyond their capabilities don't help them to develop an overall interest in education or pursue what may be their dream career. These parents should listen to their child and encourage them to succeed at something that interests them. You should still advise them to pursue education that will provide them a lifetime of security, financially and emotionally. Don't discourage dreams but keep them grounded in reality. When I was fourteen years old, I dreamed of being a professional athlete. Didn't matter to me whether it was football (I only weighed 145 pounds in high school), basketball (I was only 5'11" tall) or baseball (couldn't hit a slider), I was determined to play pro ball. Fortunately my parents encouraged me to follow my dreams but to have a fall-back plan in case it didn't work out. I got into business. If I had it to do over, with my love of sports, I might have gotten into coaching. Even parents who have a child wildly successful in a sport can't be assured they will be able to make a living playing professional ball. Injuries, competition, and opportunity, all play an important part of fulfilling that dream. Not all students want to be doctors or lawyers. Get them to focus on something that will make them both happy and successful in life.

Students

The person most responsible for educational success is the student. The old adage "You can lead a horse to water, but you can't make them drink" is never more factual than attempting to get students to accept responsibility for their own education. With some students this is not an issue as some have an undeniable thirst for knowledge and will learn regardless of their situation. Others, in a perfect environment for learning, will not put in the effort and will fail to learn. Some will excel in areas of interest and do poorly in areas of lack of interest. I always excelled in science and history but did not do as well in math and grammar while I was in school. Because of that fact, I was forced to get additional training in both math and grammar as my career path in operations management demanded it.

I have listed a few things I think would assist parents in motivating their students:

- Beginning at the earliest age, parents should stress the importance of being smart and gaining knowledge. Use training aids and rewards to excite the children about learning new things.
- Don't punish your student for failure unless it is for lack of effort. If they are trying but still have trouble, encourage

them to keep trying and get them help (tutoring, summer school, etc.)

- Emphasize that you don't have to be smart at everything. Some students struggle with a specific subject and excel at others. Encourage them to grind through the subjects they struggle with and embrace those they love. Emphasize the fact that some knowledge of those subjects they find difficult is important to their overall education.

- Based on their interests and skills, discuss career paths early so the student can start thinking about career options. Don't get excited if their first interests don't seem appropriate (my first recollection of a career choice was cowboy). They will change their minds numerous times over the course of their education.

- Don't solve all the problems your student faces. Force them to deal with some on their own. This breeds independence and critical thinking.

- Support the efforts of their teachers. *Do not* view the teachers as the enemy intent on holding your student back. I always knew that if a teacher contacted either of my parents about any issue, they would support the teacher 95 percent of the time. That certainly motivated me to prevent that communication!

Primary education is difficult as the students are growing mentally and physically during that time and face external pressures by peers and society in general. Their lack of experience causes them to believe that they will never need or use some of the skills they are being taught. Algebra is one commonly lumped in this category, yet everyone has need of this discipline. Banking/interest rates, construction and/or home repairs, cooking, retailing, and many others use algebra extensively. It is up to the parents to explain the need for the skills. The simple learn-it-or-else mandate will not get the result desired (although when all the other means have been exhausted, it is appropriate).

When students understand that they are the person ultimately responsible for their education, their retention and learning definitely improve.

Higher Education

Things change dramatically when the students move on to college or technical training. The emphasis for success falls directly on the student. Professors have little concern if you graduate or not. In all honesty it should not be their concern. Students involved in higher learning do so because they wish to learn additional skills and prepare for a career. It is on the student, as it should be, to be prepared and do the work. The concerns at the collegiate level are significantly different than grades K–12.

A lot has been said about the liberal leanings of our colleges and universities. Is this really true? Not in all cases. Although much gets publicized about left-leaning campuses, Cal Berkeley leading the way, there are a significant number of colleges with more conservative values as well. There are plenty of smaller faith-based institutions and some major universities that don't lean left. Is this really a problem? Considering that many people are more liberal in their early years and gradually become more conservative as years of experience help to formulate their opinions, I believe that this issue is overstated. I was more liberal in my twenties than I am now as some of the thoughts I had during those years have proven to be not in the best interests of the country or society in general. My oldest daughter is a perfect example.

In high school she thought that the government should take care of teenage mothers financially since they didn't have the means required to support their children. A few years later when she began working and found out how much the government taxed her income, she started leaning to a more conservative position. My only thought on this situation is that the institutions of higher learning *must* ensure both sides of issues are presented in an equal fashion so that students can make informed decisions based on data from both sides of the issue. This is not happening in some institutions. Anything less changes them from an institution of higher learning to a political activist organization.

What about radical professors who try to indoctrinate students to their way of thinking? Do these professors pose a threat? Not in my opinion. I do, however, believe that the school administrators have a responsibility to ensure their faculty presents balanced factual data and are not espousing a pure political message. Don't the schools have their hands tied by tenure of certain professors? In some cases they do, but more and more institutions of higher learning are moving away from "tenure." I believe tenure, like many other issues, has both pros and cons. Universities sometimes hide behind the tenure shield to avoid dealing with controversial professors even though most tenure agreements have provisions to terminate based on certain criteria. The real issue here is if parents are instilling core values and discussing political and spiritual issues with their children; it is unlikely that they will be swayed on a subject by a professor. They may, however, formulate their own opinions on these subjects, and they may not always agree with yours.

Financing Education

The financing of education, particularly in primary education, is based on the methods used to finance the school systems. Because the most prevalent revenue source is local school property taxes, the disparity in the financing of school districts is dramatic. Schools in Plano, Texas (a very affluent community), have significant advantage over a school system in poorer rural and/or inner city communities. The advantages of the students in more affluent communities include better facilities, newer books, newer computers/ labs, funding for extracurricular activities, and safer environments. This does not mention the caliber of the teachers as the talented teachers will gravitate to the more affluent schools and the higher salary structures they can offer. This arrangement guarantees an uneven playing field in education that is not defined by racial, cultural, or ethnic concerns but by financial means. This fact helps to perpetuate class inequity. This does not mean I think that students in either situation can or can't succeed because of this inequity. Parents and students can overcome this obstacle as I mentioned previously. It does mean that not all students have the same educational opportunity. So how do we overcome this issue? That is a difficult question as property values and tax bases are what they are and will not change.

This is one subject where I tend to be more liberal to the chagrin of some of my conservative friends. Since the local property taxes for school funding doesn't change, the only way to balance this is the use of educational funds on the federal level. The distribution of federal funds should be tied to the financial ability of the schools to spend per student. I am not suggesting that this would be an easy step or one that could be implemented immediately. It should, however, be the goal of the federal Department of Education that all students be given an equal opportunity in education. I believe that those in the Department of Education embrace this goal but are stymied in execution.

There are significant issues to face which are as follows:

- The cost to execute this plan would not be cheap. The priority of education should take precedent over many nonessential programs for funding.
- Parents who believe their school district should get equal federal funding regardless of the financial situation at their schools. Federal funding should be predicated on need of the schools, not on equal distribution of funds (that's socialism).
- School administrators who only consider the good for their schools and not for educational performance for all.

I have seen a school system build multimillion-dollar practice facilities for the football team and not allow students to take books home to study because "we can't afford to buy new book if they're lost!" This type of hypocritical thinking must be overcome. Solutions to the funding issues will take effort and time to resolve, but if we really want our educational system to be the envy of the world, we must develop a solution to this problem.

Closing this chapter I must point out that children today are more knowledgeable that at any time in history. This is largely because there is more to learn. New technologies, medical breakthroughs, and engineering marvels have been developed by students from our educational systems (and from other countries as well). My children know many things that were not even known when I was their age. This phenomenon has been going on since the beginning of humanity and will continue. My concern in education is whether or not basic skills (math, language, etc.) are taught. Using a calculator may give you the right answer, but could you have reached that same point without the calculator? Our educational system is *not* bad. Why else would we have so many foreign students traveling here to study? Could it be improved? Sure.

Economics

The economy always seems to generate negative opinions even when it is doing well overall. The problem stems from the complexity of the economic base. While certain segments of the economy could be booming, others could be suffering due to changes in public opinion, changes in technology, or a slight downturn in demand. This has been the situation since the beginning of the industrial revolution. The economy is one area where your personal view is paramount. Say you are a home builder and the housing market is booming, you are going to think that the economy is doing great. If, however, you work in high tech and it's in a slump, you think that the economy is in a recession. The simple fact is the marketplace is volatile and constantly fluctuates. There will be times of market expansion and times of market contraction. It should be noted that the expansions far outweigh the contractions. The simple fact that the population is growing will cause the economy to expand. More people mean more food, shelter, clothing, transportation, and many services such as medical, legal, and repair services will be required to keep up with the population growth.

One of the key topics of conversation around the world economy has been the rankings of the economies by country. The United States has had an unprecedented run as the world's largest economy. Is that really important? Many very successful countries have an economy valued less than the United States, but their citizens live comfortably. The total value of an economy is primarily based on the population of the country and the per capita income. One of the primary reasons the Chinese economy is now second in the world is their consumers outnumber any other country even though their per capita income is still far down the list. Couple that with the focus of the Chinese government on industrial growth, it makes sense that they would be rapidly growing. Not much is said about India, but they too are seeing substantial growth and are moving up the list. Is this a bad thing? Why would booming economies in other countries be a threat to the United States?

History has shown that growing economies feed off other growing economies via imports and exports created by the demand of the new wealth. In the 1970s it was forecasted that the Japanese economy would overtake the United States within ten years. The reality is that the Japanese economy has risen from 20 percent of the United States economy in 1970 to 25 percent in 2019. That number is down from a high in 2009 of 35 percent. Other more established economies such as those of the United Kingdom, France, and Germany have maintained their position and recorded some small gains on the United States. Other countries are moving up the list as they become more industrialized and expand their economic base. A point to remember is we will continue to see the rise in the economies as more underdeveloped countries embark on their own industrial revolution. The goal should be to develop the economies around the globe as those who are living comfortable lives are far less interested in conflict and conquest.

Family economics have changed quite a bit over the last fifty years. Many have claimed that things are tougher now and point to the number of dual-income families as proof. They want to lament that women now have to work outside the home just to make ends meet. This is simply not a true statement as several studies have shown that many families could live on a single income. They simply choose not to because of a couple of factors such as the following:

- The additional revenue from the dual-income scenario allows for luxuries such as newer, more expensive cars (and two of them), bigger homes, expensive vacations, additional spending on children in the form of music and sports lessons, private education, spa treatments, country club memberships, etc.

- Women wanted more challenge than staying home as a caregiver and homemaker. They wanted to tap their potential in the marketplace and explore leadership roles. This does not diminish those that choose to stay home in any way. Many working women opted to stay at home for certain periods to care for children and returned to work once they reached a particular milestone. My wife took advantage of this opportunity. We were one of the lucky ones.

Not everyone has the means to have a choice. Many younger people need two incomes to meet their obligations. Some couples have had financial setbacks that require two incomes. Let's not forget all the single-parent households out there today. They must and do live on a single income although some, but not all, receive assistance from the absent parent.

Family economics are better today than at any time. The home ownership rate has increased from 55 percent in 1950 to 68 percent in 2007. Families have more discretionary income than at any time in history. These statistics represent averages and is not meant to claim everyone is in this situation, only more are now.

Recessions/Depression

Nothing seems to spark financial anxiety like the threat of a recession. This seems to fly in the face of the fact that the economy has historically experienced at least one recession in every decade. The volatility of financial markets means there will be upturns and downturns and they should be anticipated. The financial impact of the recessions occurring since the Great Depression of the 1930s has been minimal in general and yet devastating to some. The problem lies in the fact that not everyone has the means to properly plan and set aside resources to ensure their ability to ride out the downturn. Recessions are particularly hard on lower-income individuals, but some wealthy individuals can face financial ruin as well.

The Great Depression of the 1930s stands as the single most devastating economic downturn in American history. Yet many who lived through those years speak of them with some fondness despite the unimaginable hardships faced by many. Why? Simply put because they lived through it. The country survived and put financial controls in place to prevent a reoccurrence of the events that preceded the crash.

To add some perspective, look at the unemployment levels during the depression and subsequent recessions:

- 1933—25 percent
- 1949—7.9 percent
- 1953—6.1 percent
- 1957—7.5 percent
- 1961—7.1 percent
- 1970—6.1 percent
- 1974—9 percent
- 1981—10.8 percent
- 1991—6.9 percent
- 2001—5.5 percent
- 2007—6.7 percent

The average unemployment rate in all the recessions since the Great Depression is 6.7 percent. That means that even during a recession, our employment rate is 93.3 percent. When you consider that the lowest recorded unemployment rate, in a nonwar year, was 2.7 percent in 1952 and most financial experts agree that the right rate of unemployment is between 3.5 and 4 percent, most of these recessions affect less than 4 percent of the workforce. If you spend any time worrying about the total economic collapse of the economy, stop. The only thing you should do is to try to build reserves that will allow you to better navigate the time period of the next recession. The recessions normally last for one to three years. For those who don't have the resources to build a reserve, be confident that you will survive it just like those who survived the Great Depression. Unfortunately, many will have to be in survival mode because they will choose to live on the edge of their means and will not have recession resources set aside.

The Government Role

Politicians like to believe that they can drive the economy to create jobs. The truth is they *can* do things to drive the economy. Job growth in the economy is driven by the creation of wealth. Microsoft, as an example, began in 1974 with two employees and today employs ninety-three thousand worldwide. The two original employees became two of the richest people on the planet. Even these numbers are dwarfed by the accumulated total of new business startups and the jobs they create. The government on the other hand creates no wealth and therefore does not create new jobs. New jobs created by the government due to expanding positions in existing government agencies, legislative mandates, and/or creating new government agencies that require hiring are paid from taxation, selling bonds, and other government fees. All these are paid for by those generating wealth. When the government uses these funds to hire people, they are in essence transferring jobs from the private sector. This does not create new jobs.

The fact is many things the government does actually reduce employment in the private sector. Every time the government imposes a mandate that requires employers to pay additional fees and/or comply with new regulations that cost the company money, they lose some ability to add workers and, in some situations, force them to lay people off. This does not mean that these measures should not be taken but that the impact on employment must be taken into consideration (and are in most cases). Don't fall into the trap that these things will crash the economy. Compromise can be reached to get the benefit without the doomsday predictions coming true. The Affordable Care Act (Obamacare) was going to do unimaginable damage to the economy, but the reality is it is still in place, and two years into the Trump presidency, the economy is booming while sixteen million have medical coverage under this legislation that previously did not have coverage.

One proven way for the government to create jobs that do drive wealth in the private sector is to fund infrastructure such as highway expansion, bridge building/repairs, investing in shipping ports, funding research and development projects that lead to new industries, and eliminating old mandates that are no longer required. Although this funding comes from taxation, it is spent in the private sector creating jobs that generate addition taxation and new jobs in expanding new industries. Investing in the country's future is always a good investment.

Jobs

One topic that always is in the front of everyone's mind is jobs. Since nearly everyone has a job or run their own business, the forecast for continued employment and the income it provides is always on the forefront of our thinking. We always worry about downturns or more importantly the future of our industry. We constantly see reports of jobs being eliminated by the changing marketplace and technologies. Is this new? Not even close. The marketplace is always changing, and new technologies have always eliminated some jobs and created new ones. In some cases new technologies dramatically improved an existing industry. The garment industry in New York City was as prime example in the early 1900s. The invention of automated equipment such as looms was set to dramatically increase productivity, but the labor force thought that the automated equipment would simply eliminate jobs. When a company tried to bring in this automated equipment, the labor force would attack and destroy the equipment to the point that the National Guard had to be called out to ensure the equipment was safely delivered into the factory. Prior to this automation effort, there were around twenty thousand employed by the New York City garment district. After the implementation of automation, over one hundred thousand were employed in the garment district as the cost of apparel dropped dramatically.

In addition, higher paying jobs were created as technicians to run and maintain the equipment were required. A major power tool manufacturer embarked on a significant automation effort that led to cost of power tools dropping and making them easily available to everyone. Their revenue and employment levels increased due to expanding sales. This is not to say that some industries haven't been eliminated or severely contracted as a result of technology changes. The invention of the automobile greatly reduced the need for blacksmiths. Buggy whip manufacturers were severely impacted as well. There are plenty of examples of these occurrences, but they are always offset by new job creation. Many times this drive for automation is a reaction to changes in labor availability and/or compensation.

A good example today is changes at fast food restaurants. In the last couple of years, there has been a lot of discussion about raising the minimum wages for fast food workers to $15 per hour. Since this became a hot issue, the fast food chains have begun installing computerized ordering stations that do not require a person to take the order. They are voluntary now, but at some point they will become the only way to order at these establishments thereby eliminating 30 percent of the employees required to staff the operation. Some would claim this is a disaster as many students and young people seeking their first job will no longer have the same number of opportunities. Think about this, remember gas station attendants? Mostly high school students who pumped gas, cleaned windshields, and checked oil. Tens of thousands were employed nationwide. The advent of self-serve pumps eliminated this position, and yet high school students can still find jobs, many supporting new technologies.

There are more people employed worldwide today that at any other time in history. It is simply because there are more people generating greater demand of more products that at any time in the past. In my lifetime I have seen a period when no one has a computer; today nearly everyone has one (smart phones are computers), cellular voice and data transmission was introduced to the widespread public in the 1980s, significantly more diversity in food services (I never had Mexican food until I was sixteen and moved to California), more energy efficient homes and cars, and many other changes that have improved our lifestyles. Each one of these changes generated jobs and wealth.

My last point regarding jobs is simply the fact that you are responsible for determining what kind of job path you will take and earning potential. If you put in the work, you will succeed.

Final Thoughts

If I have been successful, this book will cause readers to think about the topics covered and be able to formulate personal opinions based on their evaluation of the data and different points of view. It does not matter to me which side you are supporting. It does matter to me that you do your own analysis based on researched data and formulate your opinions that support your moral compass and your personal beliefs. The most important unit in our republic is the individual voter. If our republic is to remain strong, the individual voter must be knowledgeable of the issues and feel confident in their choices. The essence of life in America is the ability to formulate and act on your personal opinion. It is the fact that we can disagree and live in peace while respecting others around us that makes the USA a beacon for those seeking freedom. I disagree with President Trump on his campaign slogan: "Make America Great Again." There has never been a time when America wasn't great. There have been events in our history that weren't great, such as slavery, restricting voting to men only, Jim Crow laws, political scandals, etc.; however, our country recognized these injustices and moved to correct them.

Racism still exists in our country but has now become minimized to the point that people have made up stories of racism to further personal agendas or advance personal goals. Whites have long made up stories about blacks to deflect attention from their own actions. Blacks have made up stories for the same reasons. These people do irreparable damage to those who are faced with the pockets of racism that still exist today. We must remain diligent in our investigation and elimination of any acts of racism. We must also understand that there are racists in every race even though their numbers shrink with every new generation. The fact that Americans of all backgrounds live, work, worship, and play together every day regardless of background represents the single greatest social movement in our country's history.

The advent of social media and the expansion of broadcast news became both a blessing and a curse at the same time. On one hand we have a lot more data, on the other it has become more difficult to differentiate the "fake news" from the "real news." Even if the news you receive is biased, you can identify that bias by listening to both sides and formulating your opinion based on your beliefs. The media would have you believe that you must side with one side or the other when the reality is you can be on one side on an issue and on the other side on a different issue. The media still performs a valuable service to our freedoms and must never be infringed.

The science of today is unmatched in the history of the world. Scientific breakthroughs occur on an almost daily basis. Diseases eradicated, new technologies developed that improve our lives, and our understanding of the world around us has never been greater. That does not mean that every theory will be proven. Throughout history many theories, advanced by the brightest minds of the time, have been proven to be incorrect. Unfortunately, the drive to fund research is driven in many cases by fear, and the scientific community has embraced that strategy. Climate change hysteria is a perfect example. Some would have you believe that if we don't act immediately, the world will face catastrophic events in the immediate future. The data does not support that conclusion. A 7.5-degree increase in average temperature over five hundred years (based on current warming trends) is something to be monitored and studied but should not drive legislation that will cripple economies and/or create unfair competitive balance in the world economy for nations that elect or don't elect to adopt the legislation.

The advancement of science is a main driver for the advancement of mankind and must always be taken seriously, but scientists must be held to the lofty standards they set for themselves in the development of the scientific method. One closing note: do you really care what happens in five hundred years? I am not willing to sacrifice my standard of living on the possibility of something happening one hundred or more years from now. I don't believe that those living in the 1600s were worried about the year 2019.

Critics and experts are vital to our ability to discuss issues from differing points of view and to reach an acceptable compromise or agree to disagree. We must critically review their positions (on both sides) and determine if they have done research that supports their position, or are they espousing an opinion? It is okay for them to take either path, but it is up to the individual to evaluate the conclusions themselves. Remember that just because an "expert" has a fancy title or experience does not prevent them from reaching incorrect conclusions.

Celebrities and sports figures certainly add to the fabric of American life and, as mentioned earlier, use their wealth to support many worthwhile activities worldwide. Their opinions and political beliefs are no more valid than yours. I support their right to formulate their own opinions, but like many Americans I don't believe they are "too important to society" to not use their entertainment platform to broadcast their agendas (on either side). Let's evaluate their importance by imagining that all the existing celebrities and sports figures disappeared from the planet today. How many people would die? None. What if all the doctors disappeared? What if all the farmers disappeared? What if all the police officers disappeared? Millions would be affected if those three professions alone were to disappear. Many other professions would fall into this category as well. Don't misunderstand my position; I love my favorite athletes and celebrities as much as anyone else.

Watching Patrick Mahomes throw touchdown passes, Freddie Freeman hit a home run, Carli Lloyd score a goal for the USWNT all bring me great joy but are not vital to my survival or my lifestyle. Great performances by actors like Al Pacino, Denzel Washington, Meryl Streep, Halle Berry, and Clint Eastwood all bring joy, but they are not vital in my life. My last point here is I have yet to meet anyone who told me that their political opinions were based on the opinions of celebrities and/or athletes. They really do not have the political sway they envision. People will gravitate to those who do support their position.

The political arena in the United States needs some correction. The two existing political parties have driven a wedge in the country rather than unifying all toward progress in our nation. Both sides push a take-it-or-leave-it platform. Individually they all blame others for this scenario. Truth is they *all* own it. I would like to see a third party of moderates from both existing parties whose agenda represented the majority opinion of the American public and whose goal is to reach compromises to achieve progress. The one thing I have noticed is the politicians' view that they were elected to implement their personal values. This is not the case as they are *supposed* to represent their constituents. Too many reach office and go on to ignore the promises made to constituents during the election.

On the world political stage, I will challenge the leaders of the most powerful countries in the world to meet and team up to eliminate hunger, regional strife, cure diseases, and promote human rights throughout the world. Can you imagine the impact if Donald Trump, Vladimir Putin, and Xi Jinping were to meet and agree to each divert $50 billion dollars from their military budgets to fund programs to accomplish those goals? They would go down in history as the greatest world leaders of all time. They could encourage others to follow suit, and the world would become even a better place that it is now.

My final thoughts are we must recognize that we are living in the most prosperous and free world in the history of the planet. If we are to continue this progress, we must not let apathy rule the day. There is no guarantee our progress will continue without the involvement of all. Take the time to research and formulate opinions. Don't be afraid to share them with those around you, and *always* respect the other persons' opinion and agree to disagree. I have many friends from both sides of the political spectrum. I love them all regardless of their position. The one thing I enjoy about them is the ability to discuss these issues rationally with them. Neither of us usually will completely change our position, but we have modified our positions on occasion (it is called compromise). As I close, I wonder how many of my friends will think I am referring to them. I hope a lot.

About the Author

The author is a retired operations executive whose career began at Jet Car Wash in Inglewood, California, and culminated forty-five years later as a vice president of operations. Fortunate to have lived and worked in several states from east to west coast, he was able to forge friendships with many people from diverse backgrounds. Urban, suburban, and rural locations allowed the author to meet a cultural cross section of American society. Service in the United States Marine Corps provided additional perspective. It was these associations that helped to formulate the views outlined in this book.

He currently resides in Georgia with his wife and likes to spend time with family, traveling, shooting pool, and coaching youth sports.